YOUTH LEAGUE
SOCCER
COACHING AND PLAYING

The Athletic Institute
200 Castlewood Drive
North Palm Beach, Florida 33408
U.S.A.

Consultants

Soccer Association For Youth
5945 Ridge Avenue
Cincinnati, Ohio 45213

Demonstrators

West Chester, Ohio Soccer Players
Bill Ferguson, Coach

Technique Photos

Jump Shots, Inc.

Practice Drill Diagrams

Judith L. Bedard

Library of Congress Catalog Card Number 88-071551

ISBN 0-87670-026-1

Table of Contents

Foreword

by Vern Seefeldt, Ph.D., Director
Institute For Study Of Youth Sports

Youth Sports: Benefits and Responsibilities
for the Athlete and Coach

BENEFITS OF PARTICIPATING IN SPORTS

Sports for children have become so popular that an estimated 20 million American children between the ages of six and sixteen play one or more sports each year. This tremendous interest suggests that parents and children believe that competitive athletics contribute positively to children's development. Such a wholesale endorsement may be misleading, however, unless it is counterbalanced by the sobering statistic that approximately 70 percent of the children drop out of organized sports programs by age fifteen. Many of the children who drop out are the ones who could benefit most from organized sports if directed by competent coaches. Thus, every coach, parent and athlete should answer the questions, "What are the benefits of competitive sports for children?" and "How can I be sure that these benefits are available to all children who participate in youth sports?"

Clearly, sports can have both positive and negative effects on children, but positive results can occur only if coaches and athletes conduct themselves in responsible ways. Although many of the benefits are immediately detectable and of a short-term nature, the most sought-after and important contributions of sports to total development are those that last far beyond the athlete's playing days.

In order for the benefits of sports to be available for all children, they must be identified, valued and included in their practices and games. Following are some of the benefits that are most commonly associated with children's sports participation:

- development of various sports skills
- learning how to cooperate and compete
- developing a sense of achievement, which leads to a positive self-image
- development of an interest in and a desire to continue participation in sports during adulthood
- development of independence
- developing social skills
- learning to understand and express emotion, imagination, and appreciation for what the body can do
- developing speed, strength, endurance, coordination, flexibility, and agility
- developing leadership skills
- learning to make decisions and accept responsibilities

THE ROLE OF THE COACH IN YOUTH SPORTS

The coach of young athletes is the single most important adult in all of children's athletics. Other adults, such as officials and administrators, have important responsibilities, too, but no task is as important as that of the coach, who must guide young children physically, socially and emotionally as they grow from childhood through adolescence into adulthood.

The youth sports coach is required to play many roles. Most prominent among these are being a teacher or an instructor of skills, a friend who listens and offers advice, a substitute parent when the athlete's mother or father is not available or accessible, a medical advisor who knows when and when not to administer first aid and emergency care, a disciplinarian who rewards and corrects behavior, and a cheerleader who provides encouragement when everything goes wrong.

The age and developmental level of the athletes will determine how frequently the coach is asked to assume the various roles. Indeed, coaches may find themselves switching roles minute by minute as the fast-moving, complex nature of a contest calls for different responsibilities. The coach's responsibilities in each of the most common roles are discussed in the following section.

THE COACH AS A TEACHER

Although all of the coach's responsibilities are important, none is more important than being a good teacher. No matter how adept a coach is in other roles, these successes can not overcome the harm caused by bad teaching. What then, are the characteristics of a good teacher?

Good teachers know what they are attempting to teach and are able to **select appropriate content** for the various levels of ability of their team members. Good teachers are **well organized,** both for the long-term season and in their daily practice and game plans. Good teachers are also **interested in the progress** of all their team members, including those who are inept and slow-learning. In summary, good teachers must love their athletes and their sport so much that practice sessions and games are joyful experiences for coaches and athletes.

THE COACH AS A FRIEND

Children play sports for many reasons, but one of the most frequently cited is that they like to be with friends and make new friends. Often, the most important role of the coach is just being a friend to a child who has none.

Being a friend to a friendless child often requires initiative and extra work for a coach, because such children are often unskilled and may have personality characteristics which make it difficult for other children to like them. Often the attention and affection by a coach is a sufficient stimulus for other team members to become more accepting, too. Regardless of the effort required, the coach must ensure that every child feels accepted as a member of the team.

The coach as a friend must be enthusiastic about sports and the participation of all children. Good friends are motivators who reward players with compliments and positive instruction instead of concentrating on errors. Good friends make children feel good about playing sports.

THE COACH AS A SUBSTITUTE PARENT

Nearly 50 percent of today's young athletes are likely to live in single-parent families. Whether or not coaches want the role of being a substitute parent, they are likely to acquire it. Even those children who live with both parents are apt to need the advice of their coach occasionally.

One of the most useful functions of the coach as a substitute parent is simply to listen to the child's problems. Frequently, the mere presence of an adult listener who inserts an occasional question to assist the child in clarifying the problem is all that is needed. As a coach, you must be careful not to judge the appropriateness of a parent's actions. In most instances the problems between parents and children are simply misunderstandings about children's desires and responsibilities. Such misunderstandings can usually be resolved by discussion, persuasion and compromise. However, in situations where parental actions are resulting in physical or mental abuse, the coach should contact professional counselors who are equipped to deal with such problems.

THE COACH AS MEDICAL ADVISOR

Medical problems should be left to medical personnel who are equipped to deal with them. However, as a coach you are usually the first person at the scene of a youth sports injury and therefore are obligated to provide or obtain the necessary first aid. In addition, your judgment is likely to be called upon in situations where an injury has occurred and a decision must be made about whether the athlete should return to practice or competition.

A prudent policy for you is to resist making decisions which others are more qualified to make. You should seek the advice of medical personnel when injuries occur. Encourage your athletes to report aches, pains and injuries that are likely to impede their performance. Despite the emphasis on short-term objectives, your job is to safeguard the health of the athletes so that they are able to participate fully in physical activity well beyond the childhood years.

THE COACH AS DISCIPLINARIAN

One of the most frequently cited values of youth sports is their alleged contribution to the behavior and moral development of athletes. However, there are instances in children's sports where coaches and athletes have behaved in socially unacceptable ways. Obviously, attitudes and behaviors can be affected both positively and negatively in sports.

The first step to being a good disciplinarian is to establish the rules that will govern the athletes' behavior. These rules are more likely to be accepted and followed if the athletes have a voice in identifying them. Secondly, you must administer the rules fairly to all athletes. Desirable behaviors must be reinforced and undesirable actions must be corrected.

THE COACH AS A CHEERLEADER

Young athletes are likely to make numerous mental and physical errors as they attempt to learn specific skills. For that reason, their coaches must be tolerant of mistakes and eager to applaud any actions that represent improvement in performance.

Young athletes respond well to praise that is earned and given sincerely. Conversely, they are not very tolerant of criticism, especially when it occurs in association with a coach's expectations that are beyond their capacities or abilities. You must know your athletes so well that your requests are likely to result in a high ratio of successes to failures. When you choose tasks that are challenging but are likely to be done successfully you are in a position to be a **positive coach**. Positive coaches are likely to have fewer discipline problems than coaches who expect too much and then focus on inappropriate behavior. Being a positive coach is a good way to build the self-esteem that all young athletes need in order to feel successful about their sports participation.

THE ROLE OF THE ATHLETE

A successful youth sports experience places demands on athletes as well as coaches. These responsibilities should be stated so that athletes and their parents understand what is expected of them. Some of the most important responsibilities of athletes are as follows:

- treat all teammates and opponents with respect and dignity
- obey all team and league rules
- give undivided attention to instruction of techniques, skills and drills
- always practice and play with a clear mind
- report all injuries to the coach for further medical evaluation
- discourage rule violations by teammates or opponents
- play under emotional control at all times
- avoid aggressive acts of self-destruction
- compliment good performances of teammates and opponents
- return to play only when an injury is completed rehabilitated

Summary

Youth sports are designed to provide benefits to both athletes and coaches. However, these benefits cannot be obtained in the absence of clearly defined responsibilities. When both coaches and athletes accept and carry out the responsibilities defined in this introduction to Youth League Soccer then the benefits of youth sports participation are likely to be realized.

References

Martens, R. and Seefeldt, V. (1979). *Guidelines for Children's Sports*. Washington , DC: AAHPERD Publications.

Gould, D. (9186). Your Role as a Youth Sports Coach. In V. Seefeldt (Ed.) *Handbook for Youth Sports Coaches*, Chapter 2, p. 17–32, Reston, VA; National Association for Sport and Physical Education.

I. Philosophy

The Responsibilities of a Volunteer Coach

LIABILITY

Because they have volunteered their time, many coaches do not realize that they are responsible for the welfare of the youngsters they coach. The feeling is that because they are donating their time they cannot really be held responsible. Nothing could be further from the truth.

Morally, the volunteer coach is held responsible for any psychological damage he may cause youngsters. Parents want him to see that proper attitudes are instilled in their youngsters' minds. The physical aspect is also important. Volunteers who agree to coach also agree to be responsible for the safety of the young people they coach. If proven negligent, coaches may be held liable for physical harm incurred by players in their charge.

PHYSICAL EXAMINATIONS

All youngsters participating on the team should have a physical examination with written approval from a medical doctor stating they are physically fit to participate in athletic competition. Don't risk the possibility of serious injury because you didn't take the time to see whether the player was medically fit!

FIELD MAINTENANCE

It is your responsibility to regularly check the field for ruts, holes, rocks and other potential hazards.

PROVIDE PLENTY OF LIQUIDS FOR
PRACTICE SESSIONS AND GAMES

During exercise it is necessary to replace water loss (perspiration) hour by hour to help prevent heat exhaustion and dehydration.

HOW MANY GAMES TO PLAY
DURING THE SEASON

Many volunteer coaches get so wrapped up in the thrill of coaching (especially if it's a winning team) that they schedule extra games for the kids. Besides being unrealistic, it is unhealthy for a youngster to be involved in too many games and practices per season. Why? Here are a few reasons:

1. The strain of too many soccer games can drastically affect the overall system of a youngster during adolescence.
2. The psychological strain of winning and losing can take its toll on a youngster's emotional growth.
3. Young people must have enough time for home, school and social responsibilities. Overemphasis on athletics can spark rebellion.

KNOW THE RULES

Agreeing to coach means you also agree to know the rules. A coach who "thinks" he knows the rules because he watches soccer on television is only fooling himself. There is a big difference between pro rules and high school or youth league rules. Many games have been lost simply because a coach did not take the time to learn the difference.

How a Volunteer Coach Can Help Build Character

Using the concept that "a young person is at his learning best while at play," listed below are some areas where the volunteer coach can be instrumental in developing lifelong attitudes in the young people he serves:

DESIRE

A young player acquires the will and courage to achieve in sports.

SOCIAL CONTACTS

Young people have the opportunity to make new friends through sports participation. It also gives them confidence in the future.

DISCIPLINE

Learning to abide by training, practice and game rules teaches discipline. A good rule to follow — be firm, but fair.

COOPERATION

Working together as a team instills in young people the importance of learning to get along with others. Winning teams seem to possess this quality — encourage it whatever the situation.

EMOTIONAL CONTROL

Emotional blowups only hamper an individual's success as an athlete, and he soon learns this. Your example can be very influential in this area.

LOYALTY

Being faithful to a team, a group, a cause is an important lesson of athletics. A person will not fail himself when he has learned the lesson of being true to others.

GOOD PHYSICAL CONDITION

Healthy bodies are the result of conditioning for athletic competition.

PERSEVERANCE

The lesson not to give up is a valuable one learned when the going is tough. Young athletes can learn that slogans like "Quitters never win and winners never quit" are still applicable in adult years.

PRESSURE ADJUSTMENT

All athletic competitors are faced with thinking under pressure, whether it is a quarterback fading back to pass or a basketball player shooting an important free throw.

Care of Athletic Injuries

Did you ever stop to think that your actions in case of an injury could, in the most extreme case, save an individual's life or, in the mildest case, have your player back in action in a matter of minutes? Think about it — it's true.

The care of athletic injuries is a subject too vast and complicated to cover in total. However, our purpose in this publication is to inform you, the volunteer coach, about (1) the practical equipment you should have on hand at all times, (2) the most common injuries in youth soccer, (3) the immediate first-aid steps to follow in case one of these injuries occurs, and (4) to offer guidelines for minimizing risk and preventing injuries.

PRACTICAL NEEDS

1. Most sporting goods stores carry regular coach's first-aid kits. As a check list, however, all coach's first-aid kits should contain:

• Adhesive tape — several different sizes for several purposes
• Ammonia caps for dizziness
• Antiseptic solution (betadine)
• Aspirin for simple headaches
• Plastic bottles for carrying water
• Cold packs
• Elastic wraps of various sizes
• Gauze pads
• Soap
• Scissors
• Tongue depressors
• Eyewash solution with eyewash glass

2. Tape the telephone number of the nearest ambulance service inside the first-aid kit. Always know where the closest available phone is at every game or practice site. Also tape a quarter to the inside of the first-aid kit, in case the closest phone is a pay phone.

3. Whenever possible have a physician or nurse present. A check with the players at the beginning of the season is an easy way to determine whether any parents are doctors or nurses. If any of them are, call and ask them for help during the season. They often are quite willing to help.

THE BASIC APPROACH
IN FIRST AID

ALWAYS REMAIN CALM.

This may not be easy, the first sight of an injury can be upsetting. Nevertheless, helping to keep the injured player calm can sometimes be the best first aid you can render. This can only be accomplished if you remain calm yourself.

NEVER ASSUME THE ROLE OF A PHYSICIAN.

The old saying, "It is better to be safe than sorry," is one that intelligent volunteer coaches will heed. Whenever there is any doubt, refer to a physician.

NEVER MOVE A PLAYER WHO HAS A SERIOUS INJURY.

This includes not sitting him up.

USE GOOD JUDGMENT BY STOPPING TO THINK.

NEVER CONTINUE THE GAME WHEN A SERIOUS INJURY OCCURS.

COMMON INJURIES AND
IMMEDIATE FIRST-AID PROCEDURES

NOSEBLEED

Have the player sit and apply a cold pack to the nose (ice cubes or cold cloth) while pinching pressure at the bridge of the bleeding side of the nostril.

SCRAPES AND BURNS

Wash with cleansing solution that can be found in most coach's first-aid kits. Cover with clean gauze.

UNCONSCIOUS PLAYER

Do not move the player. Have one of your assistants call for an ambulance. Stay with the injured player and check to make sure that the breathing passages are clear.

BACK INJURY

If the pain is severe and numbness or weakness in the legs results, immediately send for an ambulance. Do not attempt to move the injured player. If the pain is slight, apply cold to the area.

NECK INJURY

As with any back injury, do not attempt to move or sit the player up. If the pain is severe, and especially if there is numbness or lack of feeling, keep the injured player calm. Many times a head injury can be a neck injury, therefore, treat it accordingly.

HEAT

Heat prostration is the inability of the human body to cool itself rapidly enough to keep up with the heat induced through exercise. In hot or humid weather the body cannot sweat and dissipate heat effectively. If there is no available source of water to replenish sweat, the problem is compounded.

Treatment should be directed at the immediate cooling of the body. Keep the player flat and move him to a shaded, cool and well-ventilated area. If the player is responsive, small amounts of water may be given until an ambulance arrives.

BLISTERS

These are fluid accumulations between layers of skin as a result of friction. If the blister is intact, use a sterile needle to make a small hole at the base of the blister and gently push out the fluid. Leave the skin over the blister to serve as a protective covering for the sensitive skin beneath. If the blister is broken, remove the dead skin with sterile scissors and soak the area in warm, soapy water. Apply a sterile dressing with some antibiotic ointment.

ABRASIONS

These are caused when sliding or falling abrades or rubs away the skin. Wash the wound with unperfumed soap and water in order to remove any foreign matter. Wash it twice a day to continue to keep it clean. Also keep the wound exposed to the air as much as possible in order to promote healing.

LACERATIONS

These are jagged tears of the skin and/or tissue. Any cut with marked bleeding should be seen by a physician. Direct pressure will almost always stop bleeding. Clean the wound lengthwise with unperfumed soap and water and cover it with a sterile dressing. Suturing may be necessary, especially if the wound is deep, if the cut is over a joint or if it is on the foot or hand.

BRUISES

These are blows to the body resulting in mild to severe pain with or without swelling. Treatments are applying ice, compressing with an elastic wrap, and elevation. Use ice if there is no pain when walking, jumping, or running. The bruise may last for a couple of weeks. If the athlete cannot walk or run or move his foot after 24 hours, medical attention is indicated. Emergency treatment should be sought if the area immediately begins to swell or severe pain occurs. Shin guards should always be worn to prevent bruises to the lower leg.

MUSCLE CRAMPS

Treatment for a severe pulling or cramping of any muscle in the body is to stretch the muscle until the pain is gone. If the cramp is in the calf, push the foot against an immovable object until the pain is gone. If the pain is in the side of the abdomen, reach your hand up as high as possible on the affected side until the pain is gone. If the pain persists, it is better to rest up and apply ice to the muscle until the pain lessens.

STRAINS

The athlete will feel a sharp, snapping sensation or pulling and will be able to point to the exact area of the strained muscle. The muscle will tighten and the athlete will slow down or be unable to continue participation. Apply ice to the area, wrap with an elastic wrap, and elevate the injured part. No activity should be performed until there is absolutely no pain in the area. One does not "run off" these injuries! In other words, once a muscle is strained, chances are it will strain again if not properly treated.

SPRAINED ANKLE

Signs of a sprain: swelling, tenderness, and bruising immediately around the front of the anklebone, along with inability to move the ankle up and down and/or sideways. Treatments are applying ice, elastic wrap, elevation. To be on the safe side, we suggest that an X-ray be taken to rule out any serious ligament damage or possible fracture. Athletes with any pain in the ankle should definitely not practice or play until the ankle is completely pain-free. NOTE: You should presume a fracture if your player is under twelve and has swelling, bruising, and tenderness over the ankle area.

TESTICULAR TRAUMA

A blow to the male genital region with or without difficulty in breathing. The player should be flat on his back with his knees bent and feet on the ground. Tell him to breathe through his nose and exhale through his mouth as if he were blowing a whistle. This should slow down the rapid breathing. He can resume activity when he is ready. If he continues to have severe pain, you will have to check and see if there is any swelling in the scrotum and if both testicles are visible. If only one testicle is detected, the other may have been pushed up into the abdomen. This is an emergency situation. The testicle can be permanently lost if not properly treated at the emergency room, ice should be applied to the scrotum if there is swelling in that area.

WIND KNOCKED OUT

Difficulty in breathing resulting from a blow to the solar plexus. Use the same procedure as for testicular trauma using the nose-mouth breathing.

GUIDELINES FOR RISK MANAGEMENT AND INJURY PREVENTION

All soccer coaches have a responsibility to help prevent injuries. Many injuries and potential lawsuits can be prevented if coaches take the following simple precautions:
- Regularly inspect your facility and equipment for hazards. Report dangerous conditions immediately and do not permit your athletes to play until it is safe.
- Warn your players of the potential injuries that can occur in soccer and point out their responsibility for the health of their teammates and opponents.

- Be sure that players warm up and stretch properly before all practices and games.
- Supervise all activity and teach strict observation of game rules. "Horsing around" is a common cause of injuries.
- Advise players about the proper playing equipment. Teach players how to prevent blisters by wearing footwear that fits correctly, by gradually breaking in new shoes, and by wearing two pairs of socks, if needed.
- Periodically check your team and players' soccer balls. Balls should be checked for proper inflation and for loose panels which could cause personal injury.
- Be sure you have express permission before using players returning to practice or games from prior serious injuries.
- Keep records and pre-plan practices. Lawsuits have been dismissed when coaches could prove orderly progression and produce records of practices, scrimmages, lesson plans, and injuries.
- Encourage players to begin conditioning for soccer three to four weeks prior to the start of the current season.
- Encourage utilization of proper technique in all aspects of play.
- Encourage proper coaching techniques by all coaches.
- Make sure that players do not play when hurt.
- Carry a first-aid kit and have water and ice on the bench at all times.
- Have a game plan worked out between yourself and all coaches on how to handle a serious emergency.
- Seek prompt medical attention for the injured player. If you do not know what to do, don't do anything — seek help.
- Consider having ice available for immediate use with an injury. Do not use ice with an individual who has any known circulatory condition.
- Prevent heat injuries by encouraging regular water breaks and by including brief rest periods.
- Encourage players to wear their shinguards at all times.
- Inform the parents about injury to any of your players. Keep an injury log all season as a safeguard.
- Get permission, in writing, before allowing players who have had an injury to return to participation in games or practices.

II. The Discipline of Coaching

A Method For Practice

It is important that coaches have an awareness of the "essential nature" of the game of soccer and that the method of presenting the skills to their players be planned to promote a genuine understanding of this.

What is the essential nature of the game? Perhaps a definition will help.

"SOCCER IS A PASSING AND RUNNING GAME OF UNPREDICTABLE AND CONSTANTLY CHANGING PATTERN, DEMANDING AN ACUTE AWARENESS OF OTHER PLAYERS AND AN ABILITY TO MAKE QUICK DECISIONS AND ACT UPON THEM WITHOUT DELAY."

If you further observe that, during a game, play is often confined to a limited space or occurs in "tight situations" demanding quick and skillful control of the ball, you have probably gotten deep enough into soccer's essential nature to decide what the priorities should be in teaching the game to your players.

The priorities, then, are the progressive acquisition of the essential skills (passing, control, dribbling and challenging, heading and shooting) and basic tactics (movement with or without the ball in realistic situations demanding the making of decisions at every stage).

The practices in this manual have been carefully selected to help the coach to concentrate on these priorities. Study of these practices will reveal that they are not "coach-dominated" drills, but realistic situations involving the players in problem-solving learning. They include:

PROGRESSIVE ACQUISITION OF ESSENTIAL SKILLS

The practices in this manual are progressive, that is, they are arranged in order of increasing difficulty, overloaded in the beginning to guarantee success, progressing to situations demanding a higher degree of skill.

A number of such situations are offered for each skill at every level of difficulty, so that the coach may add variety to the practice. The order in which the skills are presented are: 1. Passing, 2. Control, 3. Dribbling and Challenging, 4. Heading, 5. Shooting, and 6. Goalkeeping. This order is not random or haphazard. Each topic contains elements of skill and tactical awareness that are vital to success in succeeding topics. For example, success in the second topic, Control, will depend on a reasonable degree of skill in the first topic, Passing.

As you progress in your practice and your players begin to display some skill in the small-side games, it is no longer absolutely necessary for the topics to be practiced in any particular order, but, again, Passing will be the crucial topic on which success in the others will be built.

REALISM

Practice conditions should closely resemble contest conditions as soon and as much as possible. To achieve this, opposition is necessary. Activities without opposition are of limited value. They do, however, have a place in the practice. Their chief purpose is to "groove" the movement pattern of a technique or skill before it is introduced into a competitive situation. Very young players are more likely to practice such "grooving" than older ones. If this opportunity is missed, it will never return.

In this manual we have included activities without opposition, but they are linked at all times to more realistic practices with opposition. As skill level increases, practice without opposition will take up a progressively smaller amount of the practice time.

Factors That Affect the Learning of Skills

It would be convenient if the acquiring of athletic skills followed a smooth and upward curve. Unfortunately, it does not. It is affected by a number of factors which the coach should be aware of. They are:

WHOLE AND PART LEARNING

Some skills, usually very simple ones, can be acquired by practicing them whole. Others are far too complicated and must be broken down into parts. The whole game of soccer, as we have seen, must be broken down into its parts. Fortunately, these parts can themselves be interesting and are easily put back into the whole game.

The principles behind the practices in this manual allow your players to enjoy participating in realistic parts in which they can be successful and which can be related to a whole that they can also understand.

TRANSFER OF TRAINING

The progressive acquisition of game skills is dependent on the transfer of training from one situation to another. The guiding principle behind the practices in this manual is based on this transfer of training. The practices are arranged in such a manner as to promote "positive transfer effects," namely, the learning of one activity will facilitate the learning of the next.

MOTIVATION

Most boys and girls enjoy playing soccer, so there are few problems in motivating them. However, if they are to progress in skills, they must enjoy and see the purpose of practicing the parts of the whole game. Soccer, as we have already observed is easily broken down into meaningful and enjoyable parts so that the problem of motivation hardly arises.

We must emphasize the positive rather than the negative aspects of each individual performance. Situations should be planned, especially in the early stages of practice, to make your players feel successful. If they leave the practice with a feeling of pride rather than shame, they will continue to be attracted to soccer, and will be interested in discovering their weaknesses or mistakes, and be willing to correct them. What athletes believe about themselves is often more important than their actual ability.

AGE

The age of your players will have an effect on the progressive acquisition of skills. Progress for children six to eight years old will be much slower than with older groups. The important thing is not to give up. Stay with it! You will see improvement if you are patient and follow the concepts in this manual.

At about nine or ten years of age, most children really become enthusiastic about team sports and are prepared to practice hard to achieve success in them. This has been called "the golden age of skill learning" and lasts but a few years. At this age the ability to improve skills will begin to increase rapidly.

INDIVIDUAL CONSIDERATIONS

Individual differences among children will affect the learning of soccer skills. Some points to keep in mind:

1. All children do not learn at the same rate.
2. All children do not respond to the same instructional approach in the same way.
3. The greater the ideal presence of personal attributes associated with achievements, the greater the potential that will be realized.
4. Personal limitations can be compensated for. For example, hustle can overcome certain deficits in size or skill.
5. Children have different motives, values, and interest.
6. Children have different experiences and dissimilar potential for athletic success.
7. Children mature at different rates, thus producing a dissimilar potential for learning.

Pondering these individual differences is enough to make a grown person shudder. How is it possible to reconcile all these differences and somehow help every child to reach his or her athletic potential in the limited time you have to work with them? Let's be realistic. You can't. But you can think about them. You can be sensitive to these differences and alert to what they may mean in athletic potential and performance.

Planning Your Practice

Your practice should be divided into three parts:

A. **OPENING ACTIVITY**
B. **SKILL TRAINING**
    1. Small group practice without opposition.
    2. Small group practice with opposition.
C. **GAMES**

A. OPENING ACTIVITY

The purpose of the opening activity is to allow your players to begin work immediately upon arrival at the practice area. As many balls as possible, ideally one for each player, should be available so that they can (a) practice freely with a ball or (b) practice a technique suggested by the coach, probably from work done in a previous session. These are generally simply organized activities and are essentially an introductory or "warm-up" stage of the practice that leads naturally into the next part of the practice plan. There should be ample scope for free movement and vigorous activity so that the players are quickly warmed up. It is during this part of the practice that the players should be encouraged to develop their mastery of the ball, i.e., juggling, and to improve their dribbling skills. Some suitable activities for this part of the practice are noted under CONTENT OF THE PRACTICE (page 87).

B. SKILL TRAINING

This is the main teaching part of the practice. During the first few practice sessions, you will want to concentrate on a particular skill, i.e., passing, and introduce a series of progressive practices for that skill (moving from small group practices without opposition to small group practices with opposition). Each aspect of the game is then taken up in successive practice sessions. Suitable practices for each topic are illustrated and described under CONTENT OF THE PRACTICE.

It is important that practices without opposition be carried out as near match speed as possible in order to give a sense of realism and to facilitate the transfer of skill to practices with opposition.

Your role at this stage of the practice is vital. This is the part of the practice where you will find it necessary to demonstrate a particular skill or technique when introducing it to your team for the first time. A demonstration may also be needed when most of the team is making a particular mistake. If you are skillful, you can demonstrate the technique yourself. However, if you are not, you should use your most skillful players to give the demonstration. Above all, demonstrations should be good ones. They should be brief and should illustrate clearly one, or at the most, two points. They should not interfere with the flow of your plan and should always be followed by practice.

The development of skill and understanding will be determined by your ability to observe and correct faults as they happen. This manual contains illustrations for the proper techniques for each skill. You should study these techniques and practice them yourself. This will increase your ability to recognize faults and correct them.

Intelligent observation is also needed to enable you to decide when to concentrate on consolidating skills and when to progress to another level of difficulty. One of the crucial and subtle arts of coaching is knowing when to make this decision, and this knowledge can only be learned through experience. We hope this manual will help to give you that experience.

C. GAMES

Games of various kinds should take up at least half of every practice. The games played should be a natural follow-up from the preceding part of the practice and can be "conditioned" in order to focus the attention of the players and the coach on the particular aspect of the game that is being tackled. It is during this part of the practice that the players attempt to "transfer" the techniques and skill into actual games of soccer involving small numbers of players to a side. The more realistic the skill training portion of the practice, the easier this transfer will be.

DECIDING WHERE TO BEGIN

The amount of time you spend on each stage of the practice, or how long you spend on a particular skill before progressing to another, should vary according to the level of ability of your players.

It might be convenient to start from scratch with players, ages six through ten, whatever their ability, and progress quite quickly to a more realistic level. With older and more skillful groups, you can quickly access their level of skill in a small-side game.

Thus, when a new aspect of the game is introduced, about half of the time in part B of the practice will be devoted to practice without opposition and the other half to practice with opposition. As skill level rises, more time will be devoted to practice with opposition until the whole of part B is taken up with such practices. The balance will be restored when a new skill is introduced. This is a flexible plan whatever the length of your practice. The diagram in Figure 1 shows the development of the practice outline during the teaching of a skill.

If you follow the suggestions about the order of presenting the skills and use your powers of observation and knowledge of children to decide when to progress, we are confident that your players will grow in skill and understanding and gain knowledge essential to playing the game.

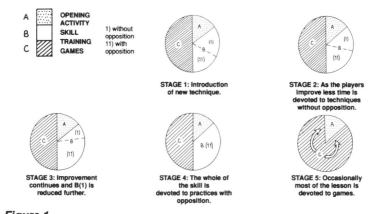

Figure 1

PREPRACTICE CHECKLIST

1. PRACTICE OUTLINE

You will need a brief outline of your practice plan to help you remember the activities that you have chosen for your practice session.

2. SOCCER BALLS

Ideally there should be a ball for each player, or at the very least, one ball for every two players. The importance of this cannot be overstated. Probably your league does not provide you with a ball for each player. This can be overcome by stressing that each player bring his own soccer ball to practice.

3. GRID MARKERS

Many of the practices in this manual are organized around the use of the grid. You will need about twelve markers of some sort to use in setting up the boundaries of the grids. The ideal grid markers are cones used by the highway departments, etc. Another excellent marker is the plastic bicycle safety flag. One can easily carry a dozen or so of these, and they are also excellent for making the small goals used in many of the practices. Plastic jugs filled about one third with sand are excellent and inexpensive. The simplest form of grid marker is a tee-shirt that can be placed on the ground to mark the grid. Of course, any combination of the above can be used also.

4. COLORED SHIRTS

Many of the practices require that the players be able to distinguish between teams. For this you will need six or eight colored shirts. You can provide them yourself, or you may want to have about half of your players always wear white or colored shirts to practice.

5. STOP WATCH

Some of the practices are timed, and a stop watch or a watch with a second hand will be useful for this purpose.

THE USE OF THE GRID

The grid is the foundation of many of the practices in this manual. It is a great method for teaching: a) execution of basics under pressure, b) improved passing, c) teamwork, d) basic tactics — movement with and without the ball.

The advantage of the grid is that it keeps the play confined to an area suitable for the activity being taught, allowing the players to "play" the ball many times under realistic conditions.

The grid is simply a confined area established by using four corner markers to mark its outside boundaries. The size is varied according to the space required for a particular activity. A large grid is sometimes divided into zones or smaller grids simply by placing markers along its perimeter. The boundaries of the grid are then imaginary lines and can be changed easily by simply moving the markers.

Figure 2 illustrates how the internal markings of a regular soccer field can make convenient grids for many of the practices.

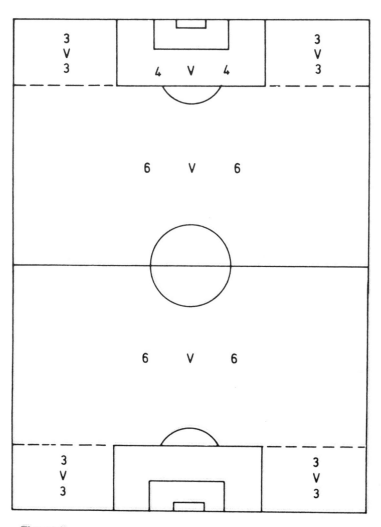

Figure 2

III. Coaching the Fundamentals

A good way to teach skill in soccer is in three progressive steps:

1. Introduce a specific technique and have the players practice it until they have achieved a reasonable degree of proficiency.

2. Introduce exercises that incorporate some movement of players and a limited degree of pressure from opponents to make the exercise related to match conditions.

3. Introduce exercises involving full pressure from opponents to simulate actual match conditions. Technique is the ability of a player to handle a soccer ball, but it does not become skill until the player can execute the technique under the pressure of match conditions.

Technique Exercises

JUGGLING

Juggling is keeping the ball in the air through repetitive touches of the ball with any part of the player's body except the hands and arms. This juggling exercise can be of tremendous help in developing ball control because successful juggling requires proper contact with the ball. Through juggling, players can work on their weaker foot and develop a good touch, balance, and concentration.

1. **ALWAYS KEEP EYES ON BALL.**
2. **EXTEND ARMS FOR BALANCE.**
3. **USE BOTH FEET, THIGHS, HEAD, AND CHEST TO CONTACT BALL.**
4. **CONTACT BALL LIGHTLY TO MAINTAIN CONTROL.**

PASSING

The coach and players form two lines facing each other and in turn roll balls to the player's opposite, who pass them back using the proper inside-of-the-foot technique.

VOLLEYING

Three players stand in line facing the server who tosses balls to each player. The players volley the balls back. The server is changed after several volleys by each player.

HEADING UNDER MATCH-LIKE CONDITIONS

The players form lines and face each other five yards apart. One player jogs backward while the player opposite serves the ball for

him to head back. The same exercise may be performed with the player who is heading the ball jogging forward.

DRIBBLING AND DEFENDING UNDER MATCH-LIKE CONDITIONS

A ball placed on the ground is the target. The offensive player uses another ball to attempt to hit the target for a point. The defender tries to gain possession of the ball, then goes on attack when he wins it. The game lasts two minutes.

PASSING UNDER MATCH-LIKE CONDITIONS

A grid ten yards x ten yards is set up with balls or other markers indicating the perimeter. A team of players has possession of the ball and must keep it away from one defender while staying within the square. The team players must move around to receive passes and elude the defender.

The same exercise may be used with two players to one defender, three players to two defenders and so on. Restricting players in possession to two consecutive touches of the ball increases the difficulty of the exercise.

OTHER TECHNIQUE EXERCISES

Other exercises can easily be devised. To make exercises more match-like, coaches may restrict the space in which to play and increase pressure from opponents. Other restrictions, such as the number of consecutive touches of the ball allowed each player, can make exercises more demanding and enable a coach to achieve specific goals. For example, a coach can force players to make shorter passes simply by requiring that all passes be below the waist.

Conditioning Exercises

Proper warmups and conditioning are vital preparation for play. The following are sample exercises for small groups:

- Each player stands to the side of a ball. With feet together he jumps laterally back and forth over the ball. For variation he may also jump forward and back over the ball.
- Each player stands with his legs straddled, holding a ball overhead with arms extended. To a rhythmic count he touches the ball to the ground next to his left foot. After bringing the ball back overhead, he touches the ball to the ground next to his right foot and so on.
- Players sit on the ground with their legs outstretched. Each player rolls a ball along the ground around his back, around his outstretched legs and continuing around his back again.
- Each player lies flat on the ground on his back with legs straight and arms stretched out on the ground overhead. Each player has a ball between his feet which he lifts up and brings overhead to place in his hands. After the feet are brought back to the ground the ball is lifted with the hands and placed back between the feet. Players assume their original positions and repeat the exercise.

Tips for Soccer Players

1. Don't dribble when you can make a constructive pass.
2. Move to the open spot — move away from your defender — so you are in a better position to receive the ball.
3. When a defender is pressed and is in doubt as to what to do, kick the ball over the touchline.
4. When the ball is lost from view, all forwards should think defensively.
5. Make constructive passes to penetrate the opponents' defense, but if a penetrating pass is not possible, pass to the side or back to a teammate.
6. Defenders can backpass to the goalkeeper as a safety maneuver. Pass to the outside of the goal mouth.
7. Make the easy play. Allow the ball to work for you. Don't work for the ball.
8. Wing forwards should stay wide and close to the touchline. This brings the defender out in the middle of the field and allows more open space for your attack.
9. Talk to your teammates on the field. Let them know what is happening in the area around them which their field of vision cannot pick up.

10. As a defender faced with two or more opponents, retreat slowly to allow your teammates to come back to help. Always mark the defender who is closest to your goal.
11. Forwards should switch positions at various times during the game with other members of the forward line; for example, center forward with winger. This sometimes confuses the defense and creates passing opportunities.
12. Never retreat with your back to the ball. Watch the ball at all times.
13. As a defender, stay between ball and goal.
14. The closer the play develops toward your own goal, the tighter the defense.
15. As a good defender, challenge only when you have a good chance to win the ball.
16. Defenders should exercise restraint and control. Let your opponent commit himself first.
17. Delaying principles are good tactics in defense. This means slowing down the opponents' forward line to re-group your own defense.
18. Back up teammates and help cover the space behind fellow players.
19. Always move toward the pass, don't wait for the pass to come to you.
20. A most important thing to learn is quickness off the mark. The first three or four steps are all-important in soccer. Beat your opponent to the ball.
21. What you do without the ball is as important as what you do with the ball.
22. Shoot first-time.
23. Play the ball, not the man.

IV. Techniques

Ball Control and Trapping

Ball Control

To play soccer a player first must learn to handle a soccer ball. Once he develops a reasonable proficiency with the ball, he must convert this technique into skill, which is the ability to implement technique under the physical and mental pressure of match play.

In developing soccer skills it is best to work first on pure technique, then hold practice under match-like conditions including a mild form of pressure from one or more opponents, and finally hold practice under match conditions including the same amount of pressure from opponents as is encountered in an actual match.

The ability to control a soccer ball is essential to playing the game. This includes not only stopping a ball or "trapping" it, but, also receiving a ball without totally stopping it and playing it immediately after gaining control. Whenever possible, a player should position himself in line with the direct flight of the ball and attempt to bring it under control with the largest possible body surface in order to minimize the chances of error.

The soccer player must be able to control a ball coming from any angle and at any speed. He must develop confidence in his technical ability to control balls quickly under all of the pressures of match play.

In the past, players were generally afforded much more time to play the ball than they are today. Players used to receive the ball, control it, look around to evaluate the situation, and then play it. Today, however, opponents pressure players far more than ever before, and thus the amount of time that a player has to control a received ball has been decreased tremendously. With this limitation of the space and time to bring a ball under control, players must not only bring the ball under their control very quickly, they must also know what they plan to do with the ball before they receive it.

After receiving and bringing the ball under his control, a player really has only one of three options: (1) he can pass the ball, (2) he can shoot the ball, or (3) he can dribble it. The amount of time he has to do any of these actions directly depends on how quickly and efficiently he controls the ball immediately after receiving it.

Trapping Balls on the Ground

SOLE OF FOOT

Face the oncoming ball with your eyes on the ball. Hold the sole of the trapping foot obliquely and wedge the ball between the ground and the sole. Keep the heel close to the ground as the ball makes contact. The trapping foot should recoil slightly on contact.

This method of controlling a ball is helpful for beginning players as the technique is a relatively simple one to master. However, more advanced players will generally utilize other techniques, such as using the inside or outside of the foot, for controlling balls on the ground.

1. FACE BALL. KEEP EYES ON BALL.
2. HOLD SOLE OF FOOT OBLIQUELY, KEEP HEEL CLOSE TO GROUND. KNEE IS BENT.
3. WEDGE BALL BETWEEN GROUND AND SOLE OF FOOT.

INSIDE OF FOOT

This trap is used quite extensively. With practice a player can trap and pass with one movement. Beginning players must keep in mind that the foot should not be lifted so high that the ball passes under it, and to withdraw the foot on contact to avoid rebounding the ball.

1. **FACE BALL. KEEP EYES ON BALL.**
2. **BEND KNEE AND POINT TOE OUTWARD.**
3. **CONTACT BALL IN FRONT OF BODY. TRAP BALL BETWEEN GROUND AND INSIDE OF FOOT.**
4. **WITHDRAW FOOT SLIGHTLY ON CONTACT TO AVOID REBOUND.**

OUTSIDE OF FOOT

This technique is used when the ball approaches from the side.

The main points to keep in mind when using it are the same as for controlling the ball with the inside of the foot — cushion the ball on contact and don't lift your foot too high.

1. **KEEP EYES ON BALL.**

2. **BEND KNEE CLOSER TO BALL AND POINT TOE INWARD.**

3. **MEET BALL AWAY FROM BODY WITH OUTSIDE OF FOOT.**

4. **WITHDRAW FOOT SLIGHTLY ON CONTACT TO AVOID REBOUND.**

Trapping Balls in the Air

INSIDE OF FOOT

Keep your eyes on the ball and your body in balance. Raise your foot off the ground with the inside pointing toward the descending ball. Speed is taken off the ball by recoiling your foot on contact.

1. FACE THE BALL. KEEP YOUR EYES ON THE BALL.
2. MAINTAIN PROPER BODY BALANCE BY EXTENDING ARMS.
3. RAISE FOOT OFF GROUND AND POINT TOE OUTWARD WITH INSIDE OF FOOT POINTING TOWARD DESCEND-ING BALL.
4. CONTACT BALL IN FRONT OF BODY.
5. RECOIL FOOT ON CONTACT.

INSTEP

This trap requires quick reflexes and often proves difficult to perform well.

Shift your weight to the nontrapping leg, bending slightly at the knee. Raise the trapping leg as far as possible from the hip while bending the knee. Keep the foot flexible and contact the ball with the full instep.

Drop your foot rapidly at first, then slow your descent as the foot and ball near the ground. This action takes the speed off the ball, permitting it to land on the ground within one or two feet of the kicking foot.

1. FACE BALL. KEEP EYES ON BALL.

2. SHIFT WEIGHT TO NONTRAPPING LEG. BEND KNEE SLIGHTLY.

3. RAISE TRAPPING LEG, KNEE BENT, TOE POINTED TOWARD BALL.

4. CONTACT BALL WITH FULL INSTEP IN FRONT OF BODY.

5. DROP FOOT ON CONTACT, THEN SLOW DESCENT AS FOOT AND BALL NEAR GROUND.

OUTSIDE OF FOOT

Shift your weight to the nontrapping leg, bending the knee slightly. Raise your other leg toward the ball with knee bent and toe pointed inward. Contact the ball in front of your body with the outside of your foot. Drop your foot rapidly on contact, then more slowly so foot and ball reach the ground together.

1. **KEEP EYES ON BALL.**
2. **SHIFT WEIGHT TO NONTRAPPING LEG, BEND KNEE SLIGHTLY.**
3. **EXTEND TRAPPING LEG TOWARD BALL. BEND AT KNEE, POINT TOE INWARD.**
4. **CONTACT BALL WITH OUTSIDE OF FOOT.**
5. **DROP FOOT ON CONTACT AND BRING BALL TO GROUND.**

THIGH

Contact the ball at the midpoint of the thigh which is raised to a horizontal level. Recoil the thigh at the moment of contact.

1. **FACE BALL. KEEP EYES ON BALL.**
2. **LIFT SO THIGH IS HORIZONTAL TO GROUND. CONTACT BALL AT MIDPOINT OF THIGH.**
3. **RECOIL THIGH ON CONTACT.**

CHEST

Always be careful to keep your arms away from the ball. With one foot kept in front of the other, arch the trunk of your body backward. Align chest with oncoming ball. Recoil on contact and let the ball fall to the ground.

1. **FACE BALL. KEEP EYES ON BALL.**

2. **EXTEND ARMS FOR BALANCE.**

3. **ONE FOOT IN FRONT OF OTHER, ARCH TRUNK BACK.**

4. **CONTACT BALL AT TOP OF CHEST.**

5. **RECOIL ON CONTACT TO TAKE SPEED OFF BALL.**

Dribbling

Dribbling Techniques

Dribbling techniques enable a player to move the ball on the ground while jogging or running. It is used to get by an opponent while retaining possession of the ball.

1. **KEEP BALL CLOSE TO FEET. KEEP EYES ON BALL.**
2. **KEEP WEIGHT ON NONDRIBBLING FOOT.**
3. **USE WHATEVER PART OF FOOT IS MOST COMFORTABLE TO CONTACT BALL.**
4. **TAKE SHORT STRIDES WHILE DRIBBLING.**
5. **KEEP YOUR HEAD UP AS MUCH AS POSSIBLE TO DETERMINE WHERE YOU ARE GOING AND WHO IS AROUND YOU.**

DRIBBLING WHILE BEING MARKED

If an opponent challenges from the side, move the ball to the leg farther from the opponent.

This technique permits the dribbler to shield the ball from the defender with his body, but it obviously requires the player to master the technique of dribbling with both feet. Players who are unable to do this will invariably find themselves losing possession of the ball far too often.

1. **KEEP BALL CLOSE TO FEET.**

2. **CONTACT BALL ONLY WITH FOOT FARTHER FROM OPPONENT.**

3. **KEEP BODY BETWEEN OPPONENT AND BALL TO SHIELD BALL.**

STEP-OVER FEINT

Feinting while dribbling is a means of eluding an opponent. Learn to watch your opponents and teammates while maintaining control over the ball.

Step over the ball in the direction of the feint. If your opponent reacts, push the ball in the opposite direction.

1. **KEEP BALL CLOSE TO FEET WHILE APPROACHING OPPONENT.**

2. **MOVE FOOT TO INSIDE AS IF BALL WILL BE PUSHED WITH OUTSIDE OF FOOT.**

3. **DO NOT CONTACT BALL — STEP OVER BALL WITH LONG STRIDE.**

4. IF OPPONENT LEANS IN DIRECTION OF STEP-OVER, QUICKLY PUSH BALL IN OPPOSITE DIRECTION AND RUN BY OPPONENT.

BODY FEINT

If your opponent takes a long stride in the direction of your feint, push the ball between his legs and run around quickly to regain control of the ball.

The key factor to remember in successful feinting is not to make up your mind about what you will do with the ball until you see how the opponent reacts to the feint. Moreover, all feints must be convincing to the opponent or he will not react to them in the desired manner.

1. **KEEP BALL CLOSE TO FEET WHILE APPROACHING OPPONENT.**

2. **STEP IN ONE DIRECTION AND LEAN WITH HEAD AND SHOULDERS WITHOUT CONTACTING BALL.**

3. **IF OPPONENT LEANS IN DIRECTION OF FEINT, QUICKLY PUSH BALL IN OPPOSITE DIRECTION AND RUN BY OPPONENT.**

4. **IF OPPONENT TAKE LONG STRIDE IN DIRECTION OF FEINT, HE MAY SPREAD HIS LEGS WIDE ENOUGH TO ENABLE YOU TO PUSH THE BALL BETWEEN THEM.**

5. **RUN BY HIM TO REGAIN CONTROL OF BALL.**

Passing

Kicking Techniques

INSIDE OF FOOT

With eyes on the ball, stride forward placing the nonkicking foot alongside and six inches away from the ball. At this point the non-kicking knee is bent slightly to allow weight to go forward on this foot. The kicking foot is turned outward. Notice that as the kicking foot swings slightly backward, it is lifted from the ground. Swing this foot forward forcefully, using a push-type action. Do not jab. Strike the ball at the midpoint for a low pass or kick. At this point the body will be leaning slightly backward at the hip. Continue with a good follow-through with the kicking leg.

1. **KEEP EYES ON BALL.**
2. **PLACE NONKICKING FOOT NEXT TO BALL AND ABOUT SIX INCHES AWAY.**
3. **WEIGHT IS ON NONKICKING FOOT, KNEE SLIGHTLY BENT.**
4. **EXTEND ARMS FOR BALANCE.**
5. **KICKING FOOT IS BENT AT KNEE, TOE POINTED OUT.**
6. **CONTACT BALL WITH INSIDE OF FOOT. TO KEEP BALL ON GROUND, CONTACT BALL AT MIDPOINT; TO LIFT, CONTACT THROUGH LOWER HALF OF BALL.**
7. **FOLLOW THROUGH WITH KICKING LEG.**

OUTSIDE OF FOOT

Techniques for kicking with the outside of your foot are the same as for using the inside of your foot, except that the toe of the kicking leg is pointed inward and the ball is contacted with the outside of your foot.

1. **TECHNIQUES ARE IDENTICAL TO PASSING WITH INSIDE OF FOOT, EXCEPT:**
2. **POINT TOE OF KICKING FOOT INWARD AND CONTACT BALL WITH OUTSIDE OF FOOT.**

INSTEP

Inside-of-instep kicking is one of the most widely used kicks. This kick can be used for cross-field passes, centers, clearances, shots, and swerved passes.

When kicking with the right foot, approach the ball from the left at angle not more than 45 degrees from the direction which the ball will take. Place the nonkicking foot about even with the ball and nine to ten inches away. To loft the ball, place the nonkicking foot slightly behind the ball.

With the left leg bent slightly at the knee and the body leaning away from the kicking foot, bend the upper portion of the body slightly forward. The upper body and the arms will help maintain balance. As you swing the kicking leg backward at the knee, turn the leg outward.

Bring the kicking leg forward with the knee slightly bent and the toe pointing outward and down. On the follow-through straighten the knee and swing the leg through, extending the kick from the hip.

1. **APPROACH BALL FROM SLIGHT ANGLE.**

2. **KEEP EYES ON BALL.**

3. **PLANT NONKICKING FOOT NEXT TO BALL AND ABOUT TEN INCHES AWAY.**

4. **TRANSFER WEIGHT TO NONKICKING FOOT AS KICKING FOOT IS BROUGHT BACK, BENT AT KNEE.**

5. **BEND NONKICKING LEG SLIGHTLY. EXTEND ARMS FOR BALANCE.**

6. **BEND UPPER BODY SLIGHTLY FORWARD AS KICKING FOOT IS BROUGHT BACK.**

7. **SWING KICKING FOOT DOWNWARD, TOE POINTED SLIGHTLY OUT AND DOWN.**

8. CONTACT BALL WITH INSIDE OF INSTEP. TO KEEP BALL LOW, MAKE CONTACT AT MIDPOINT OF BALL; TO LIFT, CONTACT LOWER MIDDLE HALF OF BALL.

9. KICKING LEG PERFORMS FULL FOLLOW-THROUGH TO ASSURE MAXIMUM POWER.

FULL VOLLEY

The volley kick is used for low drives, lofts, and for clearances when there isn't time to trap the ball. The ball is kicked while in the air before it touches the ground.

When a low drive is desired, contact the ball close to the ground. Keep your knee and body weight over the ball and contact it on the backside.

1. KEEP EYES ON BALL. FACE BALL.

2. WEIGHT IS ON NONKICKING LEG. BRING KICKING FOOT BACK AS FOR INSTEP PASS.

3. EXTEND ARMS FOR BALANCE.

4. CONTACT BALL WITH INSTEP OF KICKING FOOT. MAKE CONTACT IN FRONT OF BODY AS BALL IS ABOUT KNEE HEIGHT.

5. FOLLOW THROUGH, BEND UPPER BODY SLIGHTLY FORWARD FOR BALANCE.

HALF-VOLLEY

Contact the ball just after it hits the ground to kick it on the half-volley. Apply the same techniques as for the volley kick.

This technique is helpful when players must play a ball first-time and their run to the ball is too late for using the full volley. Proper timing of ball contact is essential.

1. **KEEP EYES ON BALL. FACE BALL.**
2. **WEIGHT IS ON NONKICKING FOOT. BRING KICKING FOOT BACK AS FOR INSTEP PASS.**
3. **EXTEND ARMS FOR BALANCE.**
4. **CONTACT BALL WITH INSTEP OF KICKING FOOT. MAKE CONTACT IN FRONT OF BODY AS BALL BEGINS TO BOUNCE BACK UP OFF GROUND.**
5. **FOLLOW THROUGH.**

BENDING THE BALL

This technique is used to make the ball swerve during flight. Contact the ball with either the inside or the outside of the foot.

1. **KEEP EYES ON BALL.**
2. **PLACE NONKICKING FOOT TO SIDE AND SLIGHTLY BEHIND BALL.**
3. **CONTACT IS MADE DIAGONALLY ACROSS BALL, NOT THROUGH IT, TO GIVE APPROPRIATE SPIN.**
4. **TO SWERVE BALL TO RIGHT, CONTACT BALL ON LEFT SIDE. TO SWERVE BALL RIGHT TO LEFT, CONTACT BALL ON RIGHT SIDE.**

Heading

Heading Techniques

Whenever a ball is too high to be kicked and must be passed or shot, it is contacted with the head. Generally, players use their foreheads when heading a ball. This is a very hard part of the body which permits painless contact with the ball and, when proper heading techniques are used, can project the ball with considerable velocity and accuracy.

1. KEEP EYES ON BALL AT ALL TIME.
2. AS BALL APPROACHES BEND KNEES SLIGHTLY. PLACE ONE FOOT BEHIND OTHER, ROCK BACK, TRANSFERRING WEIGHT ONTO BACK LEG.
3. KEEP ARMS OUT FOR BALANCE.
4. ARCH UPPER BODY BACK, THEN SNAP UPPER BODY, NECK, AND HEAD FORWARD AS BALL IS CONTACTED ON THE FOREHEAD.
5. TRANSFER WEIGHT TO FRONT LEG ON CONTACT.
6. DRIVE HEAD "THROUGH" BALL. FOLLOW THROUGH FOR MAXIMUM POWER.

JUMP HEADING

Both attacking and defending players must be able to head the ball while in the air. Especially in front of the goal, attackers will often be called on to jump and head in an attempt to score while defenders do the same in an attempt to get the ball from in front of their goal. Players who are poor ball headers will invariably find themselves at a great disadvantage on these occasions in every match. Players should practice this several times with a stationary ball held by another person or by the coach, as shown here.

1. **KEEP EYES ON BALL.**

2. **JUMP UP AS BALL APPROACHES, ARCHING UPPER BODY BACK.**

3. **AT APEX OF JUMP, DRIVE UPPER BODY, NECK, AND HEAD FORWARD TO CONTACT BALL WITH FOREHEAD.**

4. **EXTEND ARMS FOR BALANCE.**

Tackling

Tackling is the technique used to dispossess opponents of the ball in order to gain possession. When an opponent has the ball, the defender must first "jockey" or contain him until the opportunity arises to challenge for the ball.

Generally, it is best to attempt a tackle either just as the opponent receives the ball and is still bringing it under control, or as the opponent pushes the ball forward and away from himself while dribbling.

JOCKEYING

Always jockey at an angle to the opponent to force him to dribble in the direction you wish him to go. Stay on the balls of your feet with your knees slightly bent so you can make quick changes of direction.

Occasionally feint as if you are challenging for the ball. This may unnerve the attacker and cause him to commit an error with the ball that will give you an opening for a tackle.

1. JOCKEY AT ANGLE TO OPPONENT.

2. STAY ON BALLS OF FEET WITH KNEES SLIGHTLY BENT.

3. KEEP EYES ON BALL.

4. FEINT OCCASIONALLY TO UNNERVE OPPONENT.

The Throw-in

Every throw-in must be made with both feet on the ground behind or on the touchline. The ball must be thrown with equal force by both hands from behind and over the head.

STATIONARY THROW-IN

Spread the fingers of both hands comfortably to grip the ball to the side and behind the ball. Keep your feet comfortably spread. Bring the ball behind your head with arms bent, then drive the trunk of your body forward, straightening your arms as the ball's brought forward over your head. Shift your weight to the balls of your feet. Release the ball once your hands are in front of your head. Follow through with your arms pointing toward the target for a throw.

1. **GRIP BALL WITH BOTH HANDS TO SIDE AND BEHIND BALL, FINGERS COMFORTABLY SPREAD.**
2. **SPREAD FEET COMFORTABLY.**
3. **BRING BALL BEHIND HEAD WITH ARMS BENT.**
4. **DRIVE TRUNK FORWARD, STRAIGHTEN ARMS AS BALL IS BROUGHT FORWARD OVER HEAD, TRANSFER WEIGHT TO BALLS OF FEET.**
5. **RELEASE BALL WHEN HANDS ARE IN FRONT OF HEAD. FOLLOW THROUGH, ARMS POINTING TOWARD TARGET FOR THROW.**

RUNNING THROW-IN

Techniques are essentially the same as for the stationary throw-in, except that a five- to six-yard run precedes the throw. Be sure that part of the back foot stays on the ground. Learn to "drag" the back foot.

1. **GRIP BALL WITH BOTH HANDS TO SIDE AND BEHIND BALL, FINGERS COMFORTABLY SPREAD.**
2. **STRIDE FORWARD WITH ONE FOOT WHILE BRINGING BALL BEHIND HEAD WITH ARMS BENT AT ELBOWS. ARCH UPPER BODY BACK.**
3. **DRIVE TRUNK FORWARD, STRAIGHTEN ARMS AS BALL IS BROUGHT FORWARD OVER HEAD. SHIFT WEIGHT TO FRONT FOOT.**

4. **RELEASE BALL WHEN HANDS ARE IN FRONT OF HEAD. FOLLOW THROUGH WITH ARMS AND DRAG REAR FOOT FORWARD, MAINTAINING CONTACT WITH GROUND.**

Goalkeeping

Defensive Goalkeeping

The goalkeeper is the only true specialist in the game of soccer. Unlike the field players, he is allowed to use his hands and thus has to master a unique set of techniques to perform in his position.

READY POSITION

1. **FEET COMFORTABLY SPREAD, KNEES JUST SLIGHTLY BENT.**
2. **BEND ARMS HOLD OUT TO SIDE IN COMFORTABLE POSITION.**
3. **BEND UPPER BODY SLIGHTLY FORWARD, WEIGHT ON BALLS OF FEET, READY TO MOVE OR DIVE IN ANY DIRECTION.**

CATCHING GROUND BALLS
WHILE STANDING

When catching ground balls head on, face the approaching ball with feet spread and legs flexed. As the ball approaches, bend at the waist, allowing your arms to drop with palms facing the ball and fingers spread. Hold your hands close together with elbows tucked in close to your body. Give with your hands as the ball makes contact. From this point bring the ball to your chest.

1. **FACE BALL. KEEP EYES ON BALL.**
2. **PLACE FEET APART. BEND DOWN AT WAIST.**
3. **EXTEND ARMS WITH HANDS CLOSE TOGETHER AND PALMS FACING BALL. ELBOWS ARE CLOSE TO BODY.**
4. **LET BALL COME INTO HANDS, THEN DRAW BALL CLOSE TO CHEST.**

CATCHING GROUND BALLS
HALF KNEELING

Kneel on one knee, placing it close to the heel of the other foot. Behind the hands, the thigh and shin seal off the ball from the goal. Arm and hand positions are the same as for catching ground balls while standing. This method of catching ground balls may be used as an alternative to the standing technique, and is especially helpful in catching ground balls that come from the side.

1. **KEEP EYES ON BALL.**
2. **KNEEL ON ONE KNEE. PLACE KNEE CLOSE TO HEEL OF OTHER FOOT.**
3. **EXTEND ARMS WITH HANDS CLOSE TOGETHER, ELBOWS IN AND PALMS FACING BALL.**
4. **LET BALL COME INTO HANDS, THEN DRAW BALL IN CLOSE TO CHEST.**

CATCHING HIGH BALLS

Catching overhead balls depends a great deal on timing the approach and jump for the ball. As the ball approaches the goal, flex your knees in preparation for upward extension. Drive your body upward with full arm extension. Hold hands close together with palms facing the ball. Catch the ball with your fingers and draw it to a protective position.

1. TAKE READY POSITION. KEEP EYES ON BALL.
2. JUMP UPWARD, EXTENDING ARMS TOWARD BALL WITH HANDS FAIRLY CLOSE TOGETHER, PALMS FACING BALL.
3. CATCH BALL WITH FINGERS AT APEX OF JUMP.
4. BRING ELBOWS IN AND CRADLE BALL AGAINST CHEST TO PROTECT BALL.

TWO-HANDED PUNCHING

If unable to catch the ball because of interference from an opponent, you may choose to deflect the ball with one or both hands rather than attempt a catch. This strategy is especially helpful if the ball appears to be dropping under the crossbar.

Contact the ball at the height of your jump with the open palms of your hands. Straighten your arms on contact and deflect the ball toward the touchline.

1. KEEP EYES ON BALL.
2. JUMP UPWARD WITH ARMS BENT AND NEAR CHEST.
3. AT APEX OF JUMP THRUST HANDS UPWARD, EXTENDING ARMS.
4. MAKE CONTACT WITH BALL WITH THE OPEN PALMS OF THE HANDS, WITH HANDS TOGETHER.
5. PUNCH BALL OVER BAR OR CLEAR, DEPENDING ON SITUATION.

ONE-HANDED PUNCHING

Using only one hand to punch the ball often permits the goalkeeper to make contact with those balls that he cannot reach with both hands. One-handed punching will be less accurate than using both hands because of the smaller surface area used to make contact with the ball. Nevertheless, it is a vital technique for goalkeepers to master and, with practice, can be used very effectively. Always extend the fingers and use an open palm.

1. KEEP EYES ON BALL.
2. JUMP UPWARD, EXTENDING ONE ARM. KEEP PUNCHING ARM DOWN AND BENT.
3. AT APEX OF JUMP THRUST PUNCHING HAND UPWARD, EXTENDING ARM.

4. **MAKE CONTACT WITH BALL ON OPEN PALM OF HAND.**

5. **FOLLOW THROUGH.**

DEFLECTING OR PUSHING HIGH BALLS OVER THE CROSSBAR

Not every ball can be caught by the goalkeeper. Although the ball should be caught whenever possible, there are times that a save must be made by deflecting or pushing the ball over the crossbar. This situation most frequently occurs when the goalkeeper finds the ball too high for him to catch and yet still within contact range.

1. **KEEP EYES ON BALL.**

2. **JUMP UPWARD WITH ARMS EXTENDED BUT STILL BENT AT ELBOWS.**

3. **CONTACT BALL WITH FINGERS, EXTEND ARMS FULLY, AND PUSH BALL UP AND OVER CROSSBAR.**

LATERAL DIVING CATCH

Even when you are positioned properly, a ball still may be out of reach, making a diving catch necessary. In diving you must catch the ball or clear the ball with a punch. When making either high- or low-diving catches, apply similar techniques while adjusting for the height of the ball.

Drive your body toward the ball with your legs, achieving full body extension. Forearms and palms should face the approaching ball. Catch the ball with the fingers and bring it to your body. "Cradle" the ball between your arms and legs. After landing, roll over to protect ball and body from the oncoming forwards.

1. **KEEP EYES ON BALL. ASSUME READY POSITION.**

2. **TAKE SHORT LATERAL STRIDE IN DIRECTION OF DIVE AND PUSH OFF FOOT CLOSER TO BALL.**

3. **KEEP ARMS BENT UNTIL LAST MOMENT.**

4. **FRONT OF BODY SHOULD FACE PLAYING FIELD DURING DIVING.**

5. **REACH OUT FOR BALL, EXTENDING ARMS, AND CATCH BALL WITH FINGERS.**

6. **LAND ON SIDE OF BODY, ROLLING OVER ON GROUND TO PROTECT SELF AND BALL.**

LATERAL DIVING PUNCH

Whenever a ball is too far away to catch by diving, the goalkeeper should punch it clear of the goal mouth with an open palm. Whether to catch or punch the ball should be decided at the last moment, when you can best judge whether catching it is possible.

1. **APPLY SAME TECHNIQUES AS FOR DIVING CATCH.**

2. **IF UNABLE TO CATCH BALL, PUNCH IT WITH EXTENDED ARM USING AN OPEN PALM INSTEAD OF REACHING TO CATCH IT.**

Goalkeeper in Attack

Whenever a team wins possession of the ball, it must immediately assume an attacking position. Whoever wins the ball must initiate the attack. When the goalkeeper catches the ball, he must pass it on in such a way as to gain the deepest penetration into the defense of the opposition without sacrificing accuracy. Throwing or rolling the ball out to a teammate is safer than kicking it, because when kicking the goalkeeper sacrifices accuracy for deeper penetration. The main concern is not to lose the ball to the other team.

ROLLING THE BALL

Rolling the ball is a good clearing method because keeping the ball on the ground permits a teammate to gain control easily.

Always keep your eyes on the intended target. Step toward the target, release the ball on the ground, and follow through.

1. **STRIDE IN DIRECTION THE BALL IS TO GO.**
2. **ROLL BALL TO TEAMMATE AS IF BOWLING.**
3. **FOLLOW THROUGH TO ACHIEVE MAXIMUM FORCE.**

SLING THROW

Spread your fingers to grasp the ball in the base of your palm. Stride toward the target while bringing the ball behind your body with extended arm and locked elbow. This enables the arm to act as a catapult. Shift your weight to the rear leg and arch back your upper body. Transfer your weight to the front leg as your throwing arm and upper body thrust forward. Keep your arm stiff. Follow through.

1. **HOLD BALL IN BASE OF PALM WITH FINGERS SPREAD.**
2. **STRIDE TOWARD TARGET WHILE BRINGING BALL BEHIND BODY WITH ARM EXTENDED AND ELBOW LOCKED.**
3. **TRANSFER WEIGHT TO REAR LEG. UPPER BODY IS ARCHED BACK.**
4. **TRANSFER WEIGHT TO FRONT LEG AS THROWING ARM AND UPPER BODY THRUST FORWARD.**

VOLLEY OR PUNT

This method is used to clear the ball for greatest distance. Always shield the ball from oncoming opponents. Extend your arms to drop the ball from about waist height. Keep your eyes on the ball. Thrust kicking foot forward as for a full volley kick, contacting the ball on the instep. Follow through.

For half-volley or drop kick, the same techniques are used except that the ball is dropped to the ground and kicked on the bounce.

1. **HOLD BALL IN FRONT OF BODY.**
2. **STRIDE FORWARD WITH NONKICKING FOOT. SHIFT WEIGHT ONTO THAT FOOT WHILE BRINGING KICKING FOOT BACK AS FOR FULL VOLLEY KICK.**
3. **DROP BALL. KEEP EYES ON BALL.**
4. **BRING KICKING FOOT THROUGH AS FOR FULL VOLLEY KICK, MAKING CONTACT WITH BALL ON INSTEP, FOLLOW THROUGH.**

Basic Tactics

THE GOALKEEPER

The primary task of the goalkeeper is to act as his team's last line of defense. He must prevent opposing players from scoring at his goal. He must have good hands to catch the ball, quick reflexes, courage, and a sound working knowledge of the game in order to anticipate his opponents' attacks and to know when to come out of goal to attempt winning the ball. The goalkeeper controls the penalty area in front of him. His first duty is to intercept and win as many balls as he can in order to reduce the number of shots taken at his goal.

However, some shots are bound to be taken, no matter how capable the goalkeeper. Therefore, the goalkeeper must so position himself for every shot that he can cover the maximum area of the goal by diving to make the save. Whenever the goalkeeper must leave a portion of the goal open, he should make certain he has all the space between himself and the nearer goal post covered, leaving open space by the far goal post which is a more difficult shot for the attacker.

Goalkeepers must learn to narrow the angle of shooting space. If an opposing player with the ball were coming at the goal and the goalkeeper stayed on the goal line, the opponent would enjoy the maximum shooting angle. However, if the goalkeeper moves toward the opponent the angle of space available for goal attempt is reduced.

THE DEFENDERS

The role of the defenders is to prevent the other team from scoring goals. Thus, they must be adept primarily at marking men, jockeying and tackling, although in modern soccer all players should be able to perform the skills required by every position.

THE MIDFIELDERS

The midfield position generally requires the greatest amount of endurance, since the midfielders's role is to link the team's defense and attack. More than any of their teammates, they are involved in defending their own goal as well as attacking the goal of the opposition. As a result they must master both defending and attacking skills.

FORWARDS

The primary task of forwards is attempting to score goals for their team. However, all players must help defend when opponents have the ball. It is small consolation to have scored three goals if your team concedes four and loses the game. Forwards must be adept dribblers as they will sometimes need to beat defenders in some one-on-one situations and must be good, accurate shooters in order to score goals.

Team Defense

There are several types of defensive strategy. Coaches can choose to use (1) zone defense, (2) man-for-man defense, or (3) a combination of both.

In the zone defense each defender is assigned a given area of the field and is responsible for preventing successful attacking plays by the opposition in this area.

In man-for-man defense each defender is assigned one opponent to mark and contain, regardless of where the opponent may go on the playing field. When using this kind of defense, it is usually a good idea to position a free defender behind his teammates to provide them with cover and support.

A combination of zone and man-for-man defense incorporates some principles of both types. Generally, both diagonal cover and support are used in this form of defensive structure. When the ball is on the attacker's right wing, the left back marks the man with the ball while the other backs drop back in a diagonal line to provide support and cover. This prevents the player with the ball from being able to come in on goal uncontested in the event he gets by the left back, and prevents the ball from being passed behind the left back to another attacker to beat the entire defense. The following basic principles are essential for all defensive play:

1. **Delay your opponents' attack** when your team first loses possession of the ball to permit the defense to regroup and organize.

2. **Provide support** for one another as is done, for instance, in diagonal covering.

3. As the ball approaches the goal **concentrate the defense in front of the goal,** thus limiting the space available for goal attempts.

4. **Maintain defensive balance.** Never position all the defenders on one side of the field at the same time the opponents may manage to get the ball to the other side.

5. **Pressure the attacking player** in possession of the ball. Force him to make errors by limiting the time and space he has to play the ball.

6. **Control yourself.** Do not make rash commitments that lead you away from a good defensive position, or challenge for the ball during an inopportune moment.

Team Attack

The following basic principles are essential for all offensive play:

1. It is most important, of course, to **maintain possession of the ball.** You cannot score goals unless you have the ball and while you retain it the other team cannot score.

2. **Always support the player who has the ball.** Ideally, he should always have two or three teammates with 15 yards to whom he can pass the ball if necessary.

3. **Maintain as much width** as possible in your attack. Try to use the entire width of the field when possible.

4. Every pass should **penetrate as deeply as possible** into the defense of the opposition without undue risk of losing possession.

5. Attacking players should **move about and interchange positions** frequently to find space for passing opportunities and to make the opponents' task of defending against them more difficult.

6. Soccer is a quick reaction game and all players should be encouraged to **improvise** according to the momentary game situation.

7. Scoring goals often requires quickness and first-time shooting. To win the game you must **finish your attacks with shots on goal.**

V. Practice Drills

Content of the Practice

FIRST TOPIC: PASSING

Passing is the foundation on which the structure of soccer is built. Everything else that follows will involve this fundamental skill. Most experts agree that the coach should concentrate on the short pass with beginning players using the inside and outside of the foot. These are the most common passes used even in adult games. Through the "short game" your players will learn the value of accurate passing and will not be tempted to "big foot" the ball to get themselves out of trouble.

Study this manual for the proper techniques so that you will be able to recognize faults as they occur. Encourage your players to use either foot during passing practice.

PRACTICE WITHOUT OPPOSITION

1. Passing in pairs
Two players passing one ball among themselves. Use inside and outside of feet. Good opening activity.

2. Pass to each other's ball
Players in pairs, each with a ball. They take turns passing to partner's ball. Each touch counts one point.

3. Pass through the legs
Players in pairs with one ball. They take turns attempting to pass the ball through partner's legs. If successful, counts one point.

4. Pass between the sticks

Two players passing through the sticks. Stop and pass or first time pass. When it gets too easy, make the goals smaller or increase the distance.

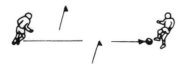

5. Passing with two balls

Two players, each with a ball, passing to each other. Can be done standing still or while moving. Good opening activity.

6. Hot potato

Six to eight players in a circle, passing the ball around as quickly as possible. Whoever has the ball at the end of the time limit is eliminated. Last player left is the winner.

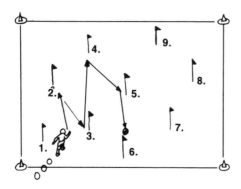

7. Soccer golf

Create a number of golf holes, using flags or cones, in a specific area. Players must hit the target at each hole. Count the strokes. Allow enough distance between starts.

8. Pass and follow
Each player must pass the ball to the target line with such pace that he catches up to the ball precisely at the target line. One point for each successful attempt.

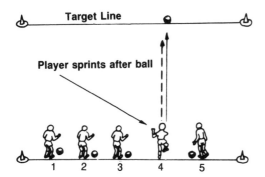

9. Pass and run to stick
Groups of six to eight players. Player with the ball passes to anyone and sprints to the empty stick.

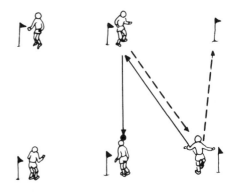

10. Pass and follow
Groups of six to eight players. Pass to anyone and follow your pass as fast as possible.

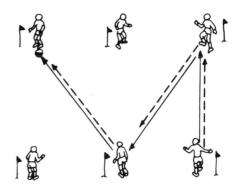

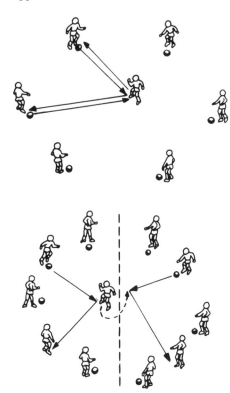

11. Circle pass
The players outside pass the ball to the man in the middle who must pass it back accurately. Can be done by stopping the ball or by first-time passing.

12. As above
But now one player on each side of the circle is without a ball. When the man in the middle receives the ball, he must control it and play it to the man without the ball. He turns and receives the ball from the other side, etc. Variation: Now he receives a ball from the side he is facing, turns and plays it to the other side to the man without a ball.

13. Pass and shoot
First line of players starts out toward the goal. Before the shot is taken, every player must have touched the ball at least once. The team that shoots (or scores) in the least amount of time is the winner. Variation: The pass cannot go to the player next to the passer, yet every player must touch the ball as before.

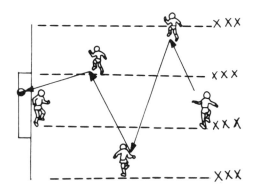

14. Pass and change lines

First player in line A passes to the first player in line B, then sprints to the end of the line B. First player in line B stops the ball and passes to the second man in line A, etc. After a while, try first-time passing.

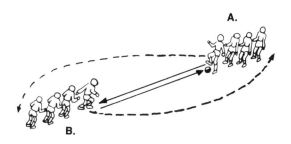

15. Four line passing

As above, but now there are four lines of players passing among the lines with two balls. Players must be alert and keep their heads up to avoid collisions.

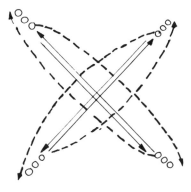

16. Wall passing

A passes to B who passes to A1 who passes to B1 who passes to C who passes to D, etc. Use one-time passing.

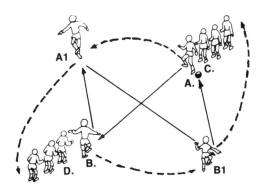

PRACTICE WITH OPPOSITION

1. Passing with two balls
Two teams of different colors, three to five players to a side in a limited area. Each team has a ball which they must pass amongst themselves. Count all the mistakes. Later, use an extra player as an opponent trying to steal the ball form either team. You may increase the pressure by adding more opponents.

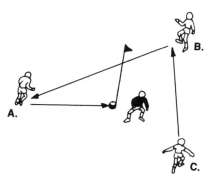

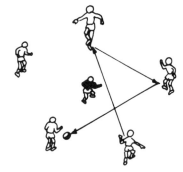

2. Monkey in the middle
Players on the outside pass the ball around without the insider(s) touching it. Can vary from 3 vs. 1 to 8 or 9 vs. 2. Good opening activity.

3. 3 vs. 1 to a stick
Three players are trying to pass among themselves with the idea of hitting the stick with the ball. The defender is trying to prevent this. Change roles.

4. Through the neutral zone

3 vs. 1 on each side of the neutral zone. A's must attempt to get the ball to their teammates and vice versa. Requires moving into a good receiving position away from the defenders. No player is allowed in the neutral zone.

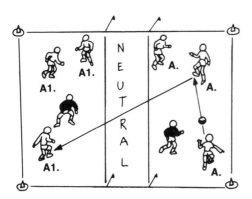

5. Mark closely

Mark a limited area with cones or flags. The defender is marking A closely who is trying to pass the ball through the cones to B. If he succeeds, the defender must turn and mark B, etc. Award one point for each successful pass. Alternate defenders.

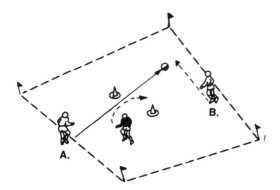

6. Through the cones
In a limited area. A's and B's are teams with different colors. Game is 3 vs. 3 and if the ball is passed through the cones, a goal is scored. A's may use the A's in the other zone for passing combinations, but all the players must stay within their own zone. You also may award extra points for x number of consecutive passes.

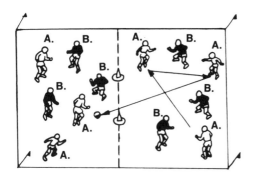

7. Soccer cones
Play any number from 2 vs. 2 to 5 vs. 5 (depending on the size of the area). Teams are different colors and each team has a 5-yard zone with x number of cones. First team to knock down all their opponents' cones is the winner.

5-Yds		5-Yds
⚑		⚑
⚑	**2 vs. 2**	⚑
⚑	**Up to**	⚑
⚑	**5 vs. 5**	⚑

8. Through the zones

In an area about 20 x 40 yards., there are four zones. A's try to keep possession by interpassing through the B zone. If B players intercept the ball, or the A's kick it out of bounds, then the B's will try to keep possession by interpassing through the A zone. Count successful through passes.

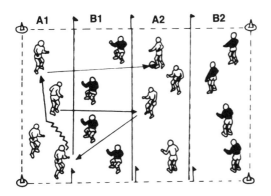

9. Wall pass game

3 vs. 3 in a limited area. Two teams of different colors. A goal is scored if the team in possession passes the ball to their resting teammates and receives a return (one-time) wall pass. On command the workers rest and vice versa.

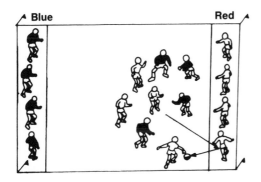

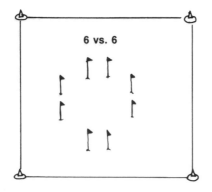

10. Four-goal game
Two teams of equal numbers and different colors. The teams can score into any goal by passing the ball through a goal to one of their own teammates. Variation: Defend two goals and attack two.

11. Get free for a pass
1 vs. 1 in the middle. the forward must get rid of the defender to be free for the pass. He now calls a name and passes the ball right back to the same person. Use a time limit, or see how long it takes to get a pass from everybody.

12. Count the passes
6 vs. 6 to 8 vs. 8 in an area about 30 x 50–60 yards. different colors. No goals. The team in possession can score a point by putting together x number of consecutive passes (inexperienced players— 3 passes in a row, experienced players — 5 or more). The object is to keep possession. If the opposing team intercepts, then try to do the same. Players may not get a pass back from the person they have just passed to. encourage players to spread out and use the entire area. Variation for younger players: Use an extra player or two, and place them always on the team in possession of the ball.

13. As above
But now add goalkeepers at each end of the field. A pass to your own goalkeeper now counts in the sequence of consecutive passes. The goalkeeper distributes the ball to one of his teammates, by rolling or throwing, to continue the count. The addition of the goalkeepers will encourage back passing and the players will become aware of the fact that the goalie is not just someone who stops goals.

SECOND TOPIC: CONTROL

Ball control is the ability to stop or change the direction of a ball coming out of the air, a ball bouncing at various heights, or a ball rolling along the ground. The ball must be controlled in such a manner that the player can do anything the situation requires: pass first time, stop and pass, stop and dribble, or shoot.

During a game, balls will be coming from all angles, speeds, spins and directions and a player is often required to bring the ball under control while under pressure, in heavy traffic, and perhaps running at high speeds or off balance.

Ball control is a skill that requires superb reflexes, balance, and body control and takes many years to perfect. Youth soccer coaches should be very tolerant of mistakes in this area and realize that skill must be developed over many seasons of play.

The types of control most likely to be used:

1. Use of the inside of the foot to take the pace off a ball rolling along the ground.

2. Use of the inside of the foot to take the pace off a low bouncing ball.

3. Use of the instep to take the pace off a low bouncing ball.

4. Use of the thigh to take the pace off a dropping ball.

5. Use of the chest to take the pace off a dropping ball.

Important points to stress while practicing control:

1. Go to the ball. If not, an opponent will get it.

2. Position the body directly in the flight path of the ball.

3. Decide what type of control to use as the situation demands.

4. At the moment of ball contact, relax the part of the body contacted by the ball, so that the ball drops softly to the ground ready for any situation.

Again, study your coaching manual for the various techniques of ball control.

PRACTICE WITHOUT OPPOSITION

1. Control in pairs

One ball between two players 8–10 yards apart. Players pass the ball firmly along the ground. They control it with the inside of the right or left foot and return it along the ground. Good opening activity.

2. Against a wall
Each player with a ball kicks it against a wall at various heights and speeds to practice control. This is an excellent activity for players of any age and they can be encouraged to practice it also at home. Good opening activity.

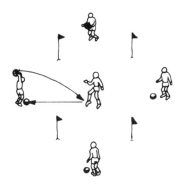

3. Control in a square
Players on the outside of the square toss different types of serves to the player in the middle. One point for each successful control. The player inside must control the ball to the ground and pass back to the server. After x number of tries, change the player in the middle.

4. Control and pass
Two lines of players facing each other about 10 yards apart. One line plays goalkeeper and tosses the ball to the first player in the other line. That player controls the ball, passes it to the next goalkeeper in the other line, and sprints to end of that line. Goalkeeper goes to the end of the control line.

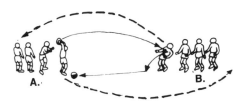

5. Control in a circle
Groups of six to eight players in a circle, each with a ball. They take turns serving to player in the middle who must control the ball and pass it back to the server. Change player in the middle.

6. Ball juggling
Every player with a ball. Use various parts of the body (instep, thigh, head, etc.) to keep the ball from touching the ground after it is tossed in the air. Have players keep count of successful attempts within a time limit. The player with the most consecutive touches is the winner. With younger players we can allow one bounce between juggies. Good opening activity.

7. Ball control relay race

Two lines of players about 10–15 yards from coaches. Coaches throw the ball to first player in their line. Players control the ball, then dribble around the flag and return the ball to the coach. First team to finish is the winner.

8. Control and shoot

In front of a goal, a line of players is outside the penalty area. Coaches serve the ball from either side of the goal. The players controls the ball and shoots at the goal. If he misses, he must chase and return the ball to the coach before going to the end of the line.

9. Control and turn

Groups of three players. Player in the middle faces player A who serves him a ball which he must quickly control and return. Now he turns and receives a ball from play B, etc. On command, change man in the middle.

10. Two-touch game

Two players with one ball. To start, one player tosses the ball up and controls it with one part of his body (head, chest, thigh, feet) and then passes it out of the air to his partner who controls it with an appropriate method and passes it back, etc. Good opening activity for older players. May be done in threes.

PRACTICE WITH OPPOSITION

It is more difficult to isolate the practice of ball control into small groups with opposition, especially for younger groups. Many ball control skills will be developed in the games portion of the practice because the players will be placed in small game situations with opposition where ball control is essential to the success of the game.

1. Control in a circle with opposition
Same as number 5 above, but now there are two players inside the circle. As the ball is served, one player controls the ball as the other one attempts to steal it. Change roles.

2. Control and shoot with opposition
As in number 8 above. But now you have a goalkeeper and when the coach serves the ball, the goalkeeper must come out and challenge the player trying to control and shoot.

3. Juggling with a hunt man
Groups of four to six players juggling the ball with one player in each group without a ball. Whenever one of the players juggling the ball loses it, the player without the ball can now steal the ball. The player who lost the ball now becomes the hunt man.

4. Control and pass with opposition
Same as number 4 above but now first player in line A serves the ball to the first player in line B, then runs to challenge. Player in line B must control the ball quickly away from the challenger in order to pass the ball back to the second man in line A. If he is successful or if the challenger gets the ball, the challenger will move to the end of line B and the controller will move to the end of line A etc.

THIRD TOPIC: DRIBBLING AND CHALLENGING

Dribbling is an important skill and must not be discouraged, because doing so would take away individualism which the players will need later on. It must be stressed, however, that dribbling is not a substitute for a constructive pass and we should use our dribbling skills to hold the ball because there are no teammates free to pass to, and get past an opponent in order to pass to a teammate or shoot on goal.

Points to stress while practicing dribbling:

1. Use your feet to push the ball gently in front of you so that you are in control of it at all times.

2. When challenged, use your body as a shield to protect the ball.

3. Learn to fake your opponent by practicing changing speed, changing direction, stopping and feinting.

4. When dribbling, practice using your peripheral vision to locate the position of your teammates and opponents.

Most children are capable, even in the early stages, of making a reasonable effort to gain possession of the ball. Until now we have not stressed challenging because the emphasis has been placed on developing the skills of passing and control. Now we can concentrate also on challenging, because the nature of the dribbling exercises with opposition require that the dribbler "take one" an opponent.

PRACTICE WITHOUT OPPOSITION

1. Follow the leader
Groups of three or four players. Use your best dribblers as leaders. The line of players follows the leader and tries to imitate him as best they can. Good opening activity.

2. Mass dribbling
Everyone has a ball in the center circle, or any defined area, and they are looking for open spaces in which to dribble as the coach encourages them to change speed and direction. Good opening activity.

3. As above, but now the coach holds up his hand with a certain number of extended fingers. The players must use their peripheral vision and call out the correct number of extended fingers.

4. As above, but on command from the coach, the players must stop the ball and place a particular part of their body on the ball (i.e., left foot, chin, right elbow, left ear, etc).

5. As above, but on command everybody exchanges balls.

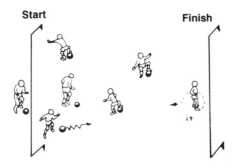

6. Red light, green light

"It" is facing the finish line while a group of players are at the starting line. When "It" calls "green light," they start dribbling toward the finish line until she calls "red light" and everybody must stop. "It" then turns around and if she sees someone moving, the player caught must go back to the starting line. "It" now calls "green light" and everybody starts dribbling again. Whoever reaches the finish line first, wins.

7. Run for your cover

In a circle, "It" dribbles around the circle, When she stops between two players, they must now dribble as fast as they can around the circle in opposite directions. "It" takes one of the vacant spots while the fastest dribbler takes the other one. The slower dribbler now becomes "It" and must stop between two other players, and so on.

8. Dribbling to the base and back

On command, everybody dribbles to the base and back. The slowest (or fastest) gets to be the starter. Everybody must hit the cone or flag at the baseline with their ball.

PRACTICE WITH OPPOSITION

1. Tag

Everyone has a ball in a limited area. One person is "It" and tries to tag the other players within the confined area. The tagged player becomes "It." Can play points or letters and words. Note: "It" must not leave his ball to tag another player, and all players must stay within the confined area

2. Kick the ball out

Everyone is dribbling in the center circle or any confined area, but now the players are allowed to kick the other players' balls out of the circle. One must not leave his own ball in order to go and kick another player's ball out of the circle. When a player loses his ball, he is out. The last player left with a ball wins.

3. Tag a player with the ball

Everyone is in a defined area but only one player has a ball to start. He tries to hit the players without a ball with his ball. Whoever gets hit must now go get their ball and join in. The number of players without a ball thus decreases, while the number of players dribbling increases.

4. Cranes and crows

Two teams have starting lines 10–15 yards apart in the middle of a marked area. Each team has a safety zone, and when either name is called, they must dribble to their safety zone. The other team must leave their balls and try to catch them before they reach the safety zone. Keep score of the most people caught.

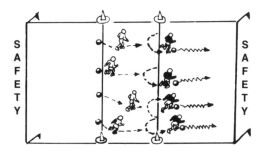

5. Get your ball

In a marked area, put two fewer balls in the middle than there are players. (Two players will always end up without a ball.) On the command "go," everybody tries to secure a ball and dribble back to the starting line. The two players who do not have a ball will try to kick away as many balls as possible. Those who lose their balls will join in the hunt. Count one point for each ball brought to safety.

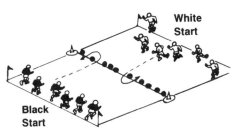

White Start

Black Start

6. Tornadoes and stars

On a regular soccer field, two teams of equal numbers and different colors are dribbling in the center circle. On command, the team called upon dribbles toward the opponents' goal while the other team leaves their balls in the center circle. The team in possession tries to score while the other team tries to prevent them. If the team without their balls gains possession, they try to bring the ball back to the center. This creates a number of one-on-one situations all over the field. An additional condition: All shots must be taken inside the penalty area.

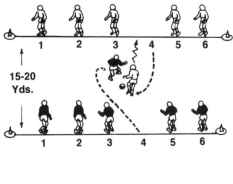

7. Steal the bacon

Two teams of equal numbers face each other about 15–20 yards apart. Coach gives players across from each other the same number. When the coach calls a number, the two players run to get possession of the ball and dribble it across their own safety line. Each successful attempt counts as a point. The ball must be dribbled over the safety line — not kicked.

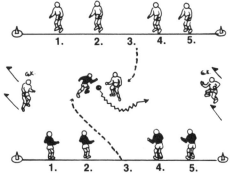

8. Steal the bacon—Part II

As above, but now there are two goalkeepers defending two small goals. When the coach calls out a number, the two players come and play 1 vs. 1 in order to score. Duration of the exercise is 20–60 seconds. The coach has extra balls to throw in. Each goal counts one point.

9. As above, but now the coach calls out two or three numbers to create 2 vs. 2 or 3 vs. 3 situations, and they can use the players on the outside for wall passes before shooting.

10. Three 10-yard squares
A player starts dribbling through the three zones trying to beat each defender, who can move from the back of his square only after the attacker enters that square. The defender cannot enter any other square. The attacker gets one point for each beaten defender, and two points for scoring a goal. (Two variations are using only two squares and varying the size of the squares.)

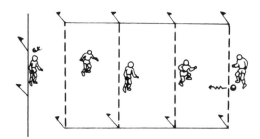

11. Faking behind the line
One player has the ball and tries to fake the defender out of his position and get to either marker ahead of the defender. The defender's job is to stay with the attacker. The defender cannot tackle the ball or cross the line. After a while, change roles.

12. 1 vs. 1
Players are in pairs with one ball. One player is dribbling and trying to shield the ball from his partner. One minute time limit. Change roles.

13. 1 vs. 1 with player resting
Groups of three players with one ball. A is dribbling and shielding from B while C is resting. When B gains possession, C tries to get it from B while A is resting etc.

14. Same as above
But now the resting player C has his legs spread apart and A and B are trying to score through his legs. As soon as the ball goes through C's legs, Player A becomes the goal, etc. Count one point for each goal.

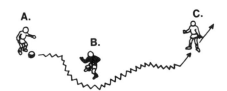

15. 1 vs. 1 to a ball
One player is dribbling and shielding from his partner, trying to hit the stationary ball. If his partner steals the ball, then he tries to hit the stationary ball. count each successful attempt as a goal. Play with a time limit.

16. vs. 1 around a stick
Player A is dribbling and trying to keep the stick between himself and player B. Player B is trying to tag him. As soon as he does, they change roles. Player B may or may not have a ball.

17. Winterbottom 1
Groups of four players. The players resting serve as goals by having their legs spread apart. Players in the middle play 1 vs. 1 and try to score through resting players's legs. On the command "change," the players change roles. If the ball is lost, the resting players play one of the spare balls in.

18) Winterbottom 2.

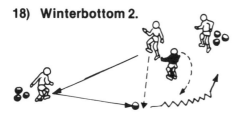

18. Winterbottom 2
Same as above, but instead of playing the ball through the legs, the workers must receive a return pass from the resting players, which counts as a point.

FOURTH TOPIC: HEADING

Heading is not an easy technique for young players to acquire. The reluctance of many children, and even older players, to head the ball can very often be traced back to painful early attempts to head a heavy ball. It is important that dry, light, well-inflated balls be used for heading practice. Fortunately, with the new synthetic materials now being used, this is usually not a problem.

Points to stress when practicing heading:

1. Keep your eyes open and on the ball.

2. Strike the ball with the forehead. the ball is hit with a forward "snap" of the upper body, moving the head, neck and trunk of the body through the ball as one unit.

3. When heading from a standing position, the feet should be placed one in front of the other for balance and power.

PRACTICE WITHOUT OPPOSITION

1. Head to your partner
One ball between players about 5 yards apart. The player with the ball holds it in front of him at head height. He heads it out of his hands to his partner, who controls it with a suitable technique before heading it back in the same way.

2. Toss and head to your partner
As above, but now the player in possession throws the ball a few feet above and just in front of his head. He heads to his partner from a standing position. His partner controls it and returns it in the same manner.

3. As above, but now the players will toss the ball up, take a couple of strides, jump and head the ball to each other. All of the above are **Good opening activities.**

4. Heading in pairs for goals
Goalkeeper throws ball to partner, who tries to head it back through the small goal. Each takes 10 attempts.

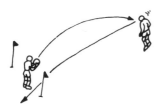

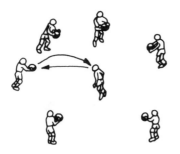

5. Circle heading with man in the middle
All players in the circle have a ball. They serve alternately to the player in the middle who must head the ball back to them. Variation: Must head it back to their feet.

6. Head juggling
Everybody has a ball. They start by tossing the ball up and trying to keep the ball in play with their heads. Have players count successful attempts within a time limit. Good opening activity for older players.

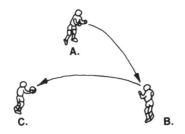

7. Throw–head–catch
Groups of three players with one ball. A serves to B who heads to C who catches. C now serves to A who heads to B who catches, etc.

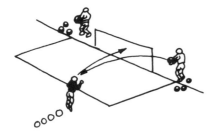

8. Head for goal
Using a regulation goal, coaches serve balls rapidly and alternately from just outside the goalpost. Players have to head for goal quickly and turn for next service. May vary distance form goal. May or may not have a goalkeeper.

9. Heading in threes
Outside players each have a ball. Player A serves ball to B who must head it back and quickly turn to head a ball from C, etc. Change the man in the middle.

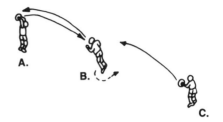

10. As above
But only with one ball. A heads to B, B heads back to A, A then heads over top of B to C. C heads to B, who has turned to face him, B to C, C over top to A. Repeat.

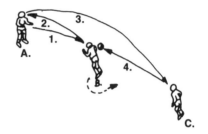

11. Heading in two
One ball between two players. They are keeping the ball in play by heading it back and forth. May play one or two touch. Good opening activity for older players.

PRACTICE WITH OPPOSITION

1. 3 vs. 1
In a square about 10 yards, it is 3 vs. 1. The server serves the ball to anyone of his colleagues so that he can return it with his head without jumping. The three then try to make x number of consecutive passes with their feet. When they have done that, or when the opponent gets the ball, the practice is repeated, the ball being served by whoever is in possession of the ball. Practice continues until each player has been both a receiver and an opponent.

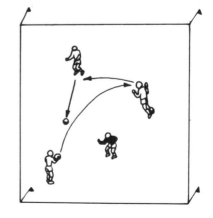

2. Head for a goal with opposition
Same as in 8 above, but now there is a goalkeeper. As soon as the coach serves the ball, the goalkeeper comes out to challenge the shooter who is trying to head the serve into the goal.

3. 6 vs. 6 throw and catch
Two teams of equal numbers and different colors in an area about 20 x 40 yards with a small goal at each end. The team in possession try to advance the ball toward the opponents' goal by passing the ball with their hands. In order to score, the ball must be headed into the goal from the pass. Opponents may catch the ball at any time with their hands and attack the other goal in the same manner.

4. Throw–head–catch
Same setup as above but now the sequence is throw–head– catch. The team in possession must advance the ball toward the opponent's goal in the following manner: Play in possession throws the ball to a teammate with his hands. Teammate then heads the ball on to another teammate who catches it, throws to another teammate who has it, etc.

The defenders may catch the ball in their hands at any time, but then they must throw–head–catch to advance the ball toward the opponents' goal. If the sequence is broken the ball is turned over from the attacking team to the defending team. Goals can only be scored with a header.

FIFTH TOPIC: SHOOTING

It is important that the players learn from the beginning to use their instep for shooting, important points to remember are power and accuracy. Study your coaching manual for the proper technique for shooting.

PRACTICE WITHOUT OPPOSITION

1. Shoot to your partner

Players in pairs punting the ball back and forth using their instep. Vary distance according to age level.  Have them concentrate on keeping their toes pointed as they strike the ball with their shoelaces (instep). Players should try to shoot into their partner's hands.

2. Half volley to partner

Use same technique as above, but have players drop kick (half volley) ball to their partners.

3. Shoot a moving ball

Players in pairs with one ball. Player A rolls ball on the ground to player B, who shoots the ball back to  player A with instep. Change roles after x number of tries.

4. Volley into goal

A line of players in front of a regular goal. Each player has a ball in his hands. One at a time, they run toward the goal and shoot (volley) the ball into the goal using the same technique as in 1.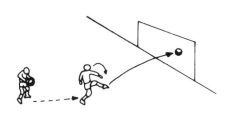

5. Half volley into goal

Same as 4 but with drop kick (half volley).

6. Shooting a moving ball into goal

As in 4 but now player rolls the ball in front of him, runs after it, and shoots from proper distance at the goal. Could now introduce a goalkeeper.

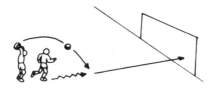

7. Shooting a bouncing ball

Second player in line tosses. the ball over the first player's head. First player runs on to the ball and shoots a goal.

8. Penalty kick contest

Each player has a ball and they take turns shooting penalty kicks. If a player misses the goal, he must sprint after the ball, and if he catches up to it before it stops rolling, he can stay in the contest. May have a goalkeeper.

9. Shoot quickly

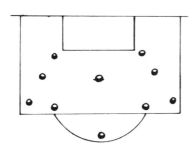

Place 10 balls at specific locations in the penalty area. One player at a time attempts to shoot all the balls into the goal while being timed. Add five seconds for every goal missed. The spotting of the balls may vary according to the skill level and strength of the players. May have a goalkeeper.

10. Pass–run–shoot

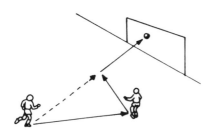

A line of players each with a ball. First player in line plays a pass to target player, who controls the ball and lays it off for shooter to run on to and shoot. Target player now goes to the end of the shooting line and the shooter becomes the target man. May have a goalkeeper.

11. Volley for goal
A line of players in front of a regular goal. First player in line moves to the front edge of the goal box. Coaches serve balls from each side of the goal and the player tries

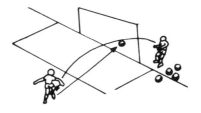

to volley the ball into the goal. Each player gets x number of tries. May have a goalkeeper.

12. Dribble and shoot
Two lines of players in front of the goal with a goalkeeper. First line of players dribble, one at a time, to the appropriate distance and shoot at the goal. Then the second line gets their turn. The line that scores five goals first wins.

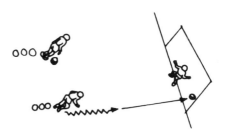

13. Control–shoot–turn
Two goals are placed about 30 yards apart. Balls are served from behind each goal alternately. Players can volley or control and shoot. Change shooter after x number of balls. Use goalkeepers.

PRACTICE WITH OPPOSITION

1.   1 vs. 1 up to 4 vs. 4 in the penalty area
Divide your team into two teams with different colors. Play will be inside the penalty area with a goalkeeper who is confined to the six-yard area (goal box). The coach has a pile of balls outside the penalty area on either side of the goal. The coach plays a ball into the penalty area and a player from each team will run to the ball

from a point equidistant from the penalty area and play 1 vs. 1, trying to score. If a player scores, or the ball is kicked outside the area, or the goalie saves, the ball players will leave and look to the coach who will toss in another. Each pair will play for one minute until all have had a turn.

Now continue the game, playing 2 vs. 2, 3 vs. 3, up to 4 vs. 4, with both teams trying to defend and score on the same goal. Variations: May require x number of passes by a team before allowing them to shoot.

SIXTH TOPIC: GOALKEEPING

The position of goalkeeper is unique. It involves quite different techniques from outfield play. Some players, from an early age, show a particular aptitude for goalkeeping, others show a passing interest before returning to outfield play. In the beginning, all of your players should be given the opportunity to play goalkeeper in practice.

The activities in the previous topics were arranged so that the position of goalkeeper could be integrated into the main body of the practice. Now you can concentrate on the specific skills of goalkeeping involving the whole team.

WHAT IS GOALKEEPING?

"Goalkeeping is the ability to provide quick, correct responses to a number of simple problems."

In general there are five areas of responsibility:

1. Dealing with shots and saves (catching and punching)

2. Dealing with crossed balls (catching and punching)

3. Supporting the defense (communication with back players)

4. Distributing the ball (punting, throwing, rolling)

5. Defending at set plays (corner kick, penalties, free kicks)

Attributes of a good goalkeeper:

Physical	**Psychological**
1. Strength	1. Courage
2. Elasticity	2. Ability to relax
3. Quickness	3. Concentration
4. Special skills (good hands diving ability)	4. Sense of game tempo
	5. Ability to read the game

5. Supple body   6. Calmness

6. Good fitness   7. Will power and confidence

GOALKEEPING PRACTICE

1. Players in pairs throwing the ball to each other to practice secure handling of the ball. One point is scored every time the ball is dropped.

2. Players in pairs kicking the ball to each other to practice punting and catching. In case of a bad kick or a dropped ball, a point is scored. Vary the distance according to the size and strength of the players.

3. As above
But now the players are throwing into a small goal, thus the players can practice diving as well. A point is scored when the ball goes through the goal.

4. As above
But now the ball is kicked. This exercise can also be done in threes. A tries to score on B, B tries to score on C, etc.

5. Save and turn
Players in threes. A and B will shoot at the goalie alternately. Points are scored for saves and goals. Players may rotate if necessary.

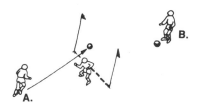

6. Turn around
Players in pairs. The goalkeeper has his back turned to the shooter (or thrower). The goalie turns around on command and tries to save the ball.

7. Push through the legs
Two goalkeepers are facing each other with their legs spread apart. One goalkeeper pushes the ball through his partner's legs. As soon as the ball goes through, he tries to turn and fall on it. Every successful fall counts as a point.

8. Shooting exercise
In front of a regular goal, at the proper distance, players shoot at the goalkeeper one at a time in quick succession. The goalkeeper must make a series of quick saves.

9. Up and down
The goalkeeper is sitting down (or lying down) at the goalpost. On command, he must get up quickly and save a thrown or kicked ball. He must now go to the other post and repeat. Duration: 4–8 balls.

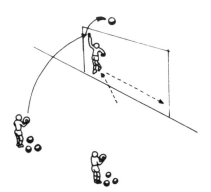

10. Post to post and over
Server 1 throws ball to near post. He must throw it high. Goalie comes to tip it over the bar, and immediately turns to go to the other post to tip a ball over from server 2.

11. Same as above, but now the goalkeeper must punch the ball. Later, add a challenging forward. The goalie must punch the ball over the challenger's head.

12. Two goalies on the goal line
The server throws a ball into the goal mouth and the two goalies fight for the ball. Each catch counts as a point. A variation is to punch the ball.

13. Shoot and follow

Server 1 shoots from about 6–10 yards. The goalie tries to make a save as player A follows in for a rebound (in case goalie misses). Now server 2 shoots and player B follows in for a rebound. Duration depends on the fitness level of the goalie(s).

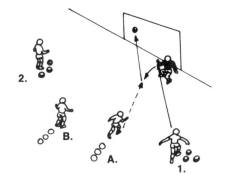

14. 6 vs. 6 up to 8 vs. 8 playing regular soccer on a small field, but with no goals. The object of the game is to get the ball to the goalkeeper, which counts as a goal.

15. Three-goal game

Two goalkeepers must cover three goals. Field players can play 3 vs. 3 up to 5 vs. 5, trying to score as many goals as possible. This will teach the goalkeepers to be constantly alert.

16. Four-goal game

In a limited area, play up to 7 vs. 7. The two teams can shoot at any of the four goals as the exercise is for goalkeepers. If a goalie makes a save, he either punts or throws the ball into the midfield.

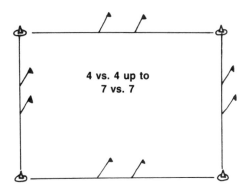

4 vs. 4 up to 7 vs. 7

PRACTICING CROSSES

The most dangerous crosses come from the goal line because this forces the goalkeeper to the forward square. This restricts the goalkeeper's field of vision tremendously. When a cross comes from the touchline, the field of vision is much better. No matter where the ball comes from, it is always the goalie's responsibility to cut the high crosses out.

On corner or goal line crosses, the goalie should stay about 1 yard off the post and 2 yards out of the net. This makes it easier to turn the ball over the bar or to go and meet the ball.

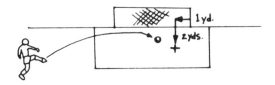

When practicing crosses:

1. The service must be realistic.

2. The coach must control the service of balls, otherwise the practice may degenerate into a pressure session with players unable to return to realistic positions because of lack of time.

3. The goalie and his defenders must be given the objective of gaining possession of the ball.

4. The coach must be prepared to demonstrate to the goalkeeper when bringing out a coaching point. (Even if in slow motion.)

Involvement off the line is undoubtedly the most difficult aspect of goalkeeping. The goalie should always try to get behind the line of flight. If he cannot pick the line of flight early, he should stay on his line.

A goalie should leave his line for only two reasons:

1. To cut down the angle of opportunity of the attacker.

2. To get the ball.

Once the goalie decides to go out, he must do so quickly. He must let his defenders know what he is going to do. He should not go out if his chances are not better than those of the other players.

When a goalie sees a cross coming, he must consider:

1. The distance of the ball from the goal. Will he be the best man to deal with that particular situation?
2. The path of the ball. Are there other players in the way?

The goalie must have superior understanding with his back players. They must always cover for each other. For example: If the ball is crossed inside his fullbacks, he must collect it, and again he must tell them that he is coming. The goalie should try to get the crosses at the highest possible point and always try to go forward to meet the ball; when he does come out, the back players should always cover the goal.

1. Crosses from both sides
Practice for 12 players, X and Y take the ball to either side of the goal near the corner and cross for A and B to score. The goalkeeper must make up his mind late and quickly to either come out to gather the ball, or to stay on the line and make a save. When he does either of these, he must now find X and Y with his throws, with C trying to intercept. Now X and Y take the ball to the other goal and cross as before and repeat.

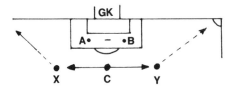

2. Reactions
In the penalty area, play 3 vs. 3 or 4 vs. 4, or whatever the coach desires. Server sends the ball across. Goalkeeper and defenders must react to the situation, important coaching points: 1. Starting position of the keeper. 2. Importance of early (correct) decision. 3. Clear, concise, confident calling. 4. Defenders' reactions when goalie goes out. 5. The techniques in making contact with the ball.

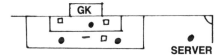

GOALKEEPING EXERCISES

1. Jogging laterally without ball. Do not cross legs.

2. Jogging backward, turning and sprinting without ball.

3. Jogging forward bringing knee up high without ball.

4. Jogging forward doing forward rolls without ball.

5. Jogging forward and changing speed without ball.

6. Jogging backward and doing backward rolls without ball.

7. Jogging forward doing forward rolls with ball.

8. Hopping while bouncing ball with both hands waist high.

9. Hopping while bouncing ball around body, exchanging hands.

10. Holding ball head high, dropping it and catching it at shoe tops level.

11. Tossing ball between legs up into the air, turning, and catching it.

12. Rolling ball on ground around spread legs while standing.

13. Rolling ball on ground around outstretched legs while sitting.

14. Rolling ball on ground from side to side under chest while lying on stomach.

15. Receiving ball tossed at various directions while standing.

16. Receiving ball on both sides while sitting.

17. Receiving ball on both sides while crouched, diving to save.

18. Receiving ball on both sides while kneeling.

19. Receiving ball on both sides while standing. Diving to save.

20. Ball rolled through the legs from front, turning and diving on it.

21. 2 GK, 2 balls, close range. One tosses and one rolls ball...at each other.

22. 2 GK, 1 ball, close range, Kicking and throwing ball at each other.

23. Punting and catching against a kickboard using both feet.

24. 2 GK, 1 ball. distance punting ball to each other.

25. Receiving at highest point in front of goal.

26. Kicking goal kick off ground.

27. Tapping a crossed ball over goal.

28. Punching away a crossed ball.

29. GK vs. attacker approaching the goal with the ball.

30. Leaving goal to receive high crossed ball.

31. Using feet to stop shots at goal.

GAMES

The Games portion of the practice should be a natural extension of the Skill portion, so that there is a possibility of transferring techniques into game situations, in general, rules should be keep to a minimum. The important thing is the "spirit of the game."

SMALL SIDE SCRIMMAGE GAME

Basic rules

1. Divide your players into two teams of different colors, six to eight to a side, of equal ability (as near as possible).

2. Playing field is about 30 x 60 yards with goals 12 yards wide made of cones or flags. Mark a goal area in a semicircle of 20 foot radius using tee-shirts or any suitable material.

3. No offsides.

4. Normal throw-ins can be taken, or the ball can be side-footed or rolled along the ground into play.

5. The game commences by the ball being thrown out by one of the goalkeepers. When a goal is scored, the game begins again in the same way.

6. A ball played over the goal line, by an attacker or defender, is returned to play by the goalkeeper rolling it with an underarm action.

7. Only the defending goalkeeper is allowed inside his own goal area, and he may handle the ball only in this area.

   Penalty for infringement:

   a) by the defense — a penalty kick.

   b) By the attacking team — a free kick at the point of entry into the circle.

8. All other infringements — indirect free kick.

9. A goal can be scored from anywhere outside the goal area.

10. Charging is forbidden.

11. The game is controlled by a referee, who may be the coach or one of the players. Allow no arguing with the referee's calls.

"CONDITIONED" GAMES

The small side scrimmage game can also be "conditioned" so that the attention of the players is focused on a particular aspect of the game. Only one condition should be used at a time and only for about five minutes. The conditions imposed can be related to a particular skill being taught. Here are some examples:

Passing

1. The ball must not go above waist height. This insures that the ball is played with the feet.

2. A player can only touch the ball twice before passing it. This condition prevents a player from holding on to the ball too long and will cause his teammates to run into open space to receive a pass.

3. The ball must be passed with the inside of the foot.

4. The ball must be passed with the outside of the foot.

5. No pass should be more than 5 yards. This cuts out long, aimless passes.

Penalty for infringement of any of the above: indirect free kick.

Dribbling and Challenging

1. The player in possession must "take on" an opponent, trying to beat him before passing or shooting. This condition will obviously encourage challenging.

Penalty for infringement: indirect free kick.

Heading

1. A goal can only be scored with a header.

2. All returns to the field must be made with a header — including corners and goal kicks.

Penalty for infringement: indirect free kick.

Basic Tactics

1. A player must never stand still after he has passed the ball.
2. The passer of the ball must call "hold" or "pass" to the receiver.

Penalty for infringement: indirect free kick.

OTHER GAMES

There are numerous games that include techniques from soccer or other games that can be played to increase the general level of skill and tactical answers. Here are a few:

1. **Soccer baseball**
   Two teams of equal numbers. Home plate is in front of the goal. Bases are placed according to the age of the players. Pitcher passes or rolls the ball to the batter who kicks the ball (practice instep kicking) to the outfield and proceeds around the bases as in baseball.
   Batter tries to run all the bases before the outfielders score into the goal (home plate). Outfielders can get the runner out only by scoring a goal. May use a goalkeeper. Three outs and change sides.

2. **Soccer tennis**
   The net can be a piece of string or rope about three or four feet high, between two posts, or you can play 4 vs. 4 on a regular tennis court. The rules can be made to suit the skill level of the players. In its simplest form, the ball is allowed to bounce once before it is returned with any part of the body except the hands. It can, however, be modified to allow two or three contacts on one side with or without a bounce between each contact. The game is started with an underhand throw from the baseline and can be played by any of the receiving team.

3. **Heading tennis**
   This game is played with a team of four to six using the same size court, but raising the (net) to 4 or 6 feet. Only headers can be used. Again, the rules can be made to suit the ability of the players. The ball can be returned the first time or it can be headed two or three times before being returned. A light plastic ball can be used for younger players.

4. **Extra player games**
   In these games, an extra player joins whichever side has possession of the ball. Thus, in a small side scrimmage game. the team in possession loses. its extra player(s) to the other side as soon as they are successfully challenged. With less skillful players, there can be as many as three extra players. This game helps convince the players of the importance of good passing and control to retain possession of the ball.

5. Uneven team games

Sides of uneven size play each other but have different targets. For example, in a 4 vs. 2 game, the four might be asked either (a) to attach a smaller goal or (b) to score in a more difficult way, e.g., to control the ball over their opponents' goal line while their opponents score normally. This game again stresses the importance of possession and the importance of the outnumbered team containing or jockeying its opponents.

INDIVIDUAL SKILL DEVELOPMENT PROGRAM

(This program can be given to individual players to use at home to continue their skill development.)

A daily program like this will improve your techniques tremendously. You will find that constant repetition is the key to improving your skills.

Allow one minute for each of the flowing exercises:

1. **Head juggling**
2. **Dribbling** — Practice tight ball control. (Keep the ball close.)
3. **Thigh juggling**
4. **Dribbling** — Practice changing directions quickly.
5. **Instep juggling**
6. **Dribbling** — Practice changing speeds — start slowly and accelerate for a distance of 10 yards, and then go slowly again.
7. **Combined juggling** — Combine head, thigh, and instep juggling.
8. **Dribbling** — Combine change of direction and speed.

After doing each of the above exercises for one minute, start over and repeat each exercise for one minute more.

Now spend 10 minutes working on ball control. Throw or kick the ball against a wall. control the ball on return and repeat. If you have a partner, have him throw or kick the ball to you.

Work 15 minutes on all types of passing. Set up targets at 10-yard, 20-yard, and 30-yard distance. (Chairs, shirts, rocks, etc. can be used as targets.) Start passing stationary balls to the targets, and then dribble to a spot and pass while moving. Use both your left and right feet to pass.

Work 10 minutes on heading. Head the ball against a wall. Strive to keep it in motion; count the number of repetitions and try to improve every day. Stand close to wall while heading.

Work 10 minutes on dribbling. Set up an obstacle course using trees, shirts, cones, etc. and dribble around them. Strive for top speed and ball control while dribbling.

Basic Team Tactics

The word tactics is one of the most misunderstood words relating to soccer. Some people will read a book which delves into such tactical maneuvers as "crossover plays," "overlapping half or fullbacks," "diagonal runs," and so on. They mistakenly want to try these with youth teams. Even some of the best college teams cannot execute such tactics. A simple give and go pass is a tactic. A three on one is a tactic. Proper defensive coverage falls into the area of tactics. Soccer is a simple game. Keep it that way. Let your team develop through the fundamentals and expand your use of tactics as both you and they develop.

THE PRINCIPLES OF ATTACK

(As you might relate it to your team.)

Our attack starts at the moment when any player on our team gets the ball, e.g., the goalkeeper, or any other player for the kick off, free kick, throw-in, corner ball, or the first pass.

Our first pass is as important as our last pass and must be well prepared, because our attack begins with the first pass and has to be finished by the last pass and final goal shot.

A successful attack will develop step by step according to the following pattern:

1.	Running into open space	MOBILITY
2.	Playing without the ball	MOBILITY
3.	Combination of play	DEPTH, WIDTH, PENETRATION
4.	Dribbling	IMPROVISATION
5.	Goal shot	FINISHING

1. Running into open space
There are "dead" spaces and open spaces during play. In order to keep the ball for our team, every player has to run out of the "dead" spaces into the open space. Mobility keeps the ball moving. Nobody is faster than the ball and nobody has better endurance. "Use the ball" is still the best advice for every attack.

If you are trying to improve your peripheral sight, and looking around and thinking in advance, you will find the open space and will be prepared for every necessary action.

2. Playing without the ball
Running free into open space is, of course, playing without the ball. But, in general, the player who runs free wants to receive the ball. Therefore, we differentiate between these two actions. Obviously, every player who is running to open space cannot get the ball, but a smart player knows many tricky ways to drag an opponent away and to open the space for a teammate. This is playing without the ball.

3. Combination play
Running free into open space and playing without the ball is the preparation of combination play. According to the organization of our opponents' defense, there are two different ways we can attack.

1. If our opponents are well prepared to stop our attack, we will have to use the midfield and keep the ball until we find open spaces for successful through passes

2. If our opponents' defense is less well organized, we shall use a fast counterattack to beat them.

4. Dribbling (Improvisation)
Our match practice has been teaching us three kinds of dribbling. 1. To hold the ball until a teammate is in a free position to receive a pass. 2. To dribble, beat your opponent, and drag your teammate's opponent along, thus playing your teammate free. 3. To beat one or two opponents and score, or let a teammate score.

5. Goal shot
Everything we have done so far is nothing without finishing. There is no substitute for goals.

PRINCIPLES OF DEFENSE

(As you might relate it to your team.)

Our defense is the necessary stronghold from which our attack can be started. If we are weak in defense, we obviously cannot stop our opponent; furthermore, we cannot control the pace of the game, and we cannot launch successful attacks.

Our defense starts at the moment when any player on our team has lost the ball. A well-organized defense is developing step by step in the following pattern:

1. Immediate chase   DELAY
2. Fall back
3. Man to man   CONCENTRATION, BALANCE
4. Zone defense
5. Attack man and ball   CONTROL RESTRAINT

1. Immediate chase

It is human nature that a player who has lost the ball wants to take a break, but players who rest on defense or attack are no longer useful teammates. The valuable team player has to do his job, both on attack and defense, without a break. That means, he must chase immediately after his opponent. Maybe you will get the ball back; maybe you will make your opponent nervous, and the result is a mispass; but in any case, you engage him in a duel and your team wins time.

2. Fall Back

After our team has lost the ball, our forwards are our first defenders. They have to chase immediately after their opponents.

The next defenders are our midfielders (halfbacks). Their job is to delay the opposite attack. They are moving back as fast as shooting distance to lure their opponents to waste time in the midfield. At this time, the defense gets organized for the coming battle.

3. Man to man

In shooting distance, man-to-man marking and organized zone defense are prepared. The closer the ball comes to your man, the tighter you must make him. The farther the ball is away, the more distance is allowed between yourself and your opponent.

A back player has to control the man and the ball. He has to stay between his man and the goal, and he must be sure that all passes toward his opponent are running in front of him and not into open space behind his back.

If possible, a back player tries to get the ball before his opponent, but at least he attacks the forward at the moment of ball contact. If both actions are impossible, the back player has to show all his skill and class to stop the forward with the ball.

Summary of the position of back players:

MATCH	1.	Defensive player must always watch over opponent and ball.
STAY	2.	Always stay between man and goal (line up with the ball and goal).
	3.	Every pass to your man has to run in front of you (not into spaces behind you, which are on your blind side).
FIRST AIM	4.	If there is a pass to your man, stay back and try to intercept.
SECOND AIM	5.	Tackle as soon as he gets it, at his weakest moment. don't act carelessly.
THIRD AIM	6.	Challenge him with your best. Force him to sideline.

4. Zone defense

In general, a well-organized defense marks man to man on the ball-side of the field, and covers the other side. The combination of man-to-man marking and covering is the best way to organize a defense effectively. That means that every defender controls, at all times, both the man and the ball, and is prepared to cover for his teammate.

Tight man-to-man marking is sometimes very important but not always very difficult. Clever zone defense needs more ability, experience, and training.

An organized, concentrated, and well balanced defense within shooting distance around the goal is hard to beat.

5. Attack man and ball

The best back players are not only robust and tough, but also clever and masters of feinting. If necessary, they attack resolutely and vigorously. In other situations, they prepare traps for the forwards and snatch the ball away, sometimes without body contact. Good defenders will never attack blindly. They are masters of what we call timing, control, and restraint.

As soon as our defenders have the ball, they start immediately for a promising counterattack.

VI. Systems of Play

Team Play

In selecting a system, the formation must be compatible with the players. A coach should never attempt to force a particular formation on his players. Also, a formation is not rigidly held throughout the game. It is only a framework through which different plays are worked. After each play has terminated, the players move back into formation.

Soccer is played with the men positioned in a series of inter-locking triangles which add depth to both the offense and defense. This means that forwards and defense men must not attack or defend on a "flat front." In a situation where three backs stand in a straight line across the field, none of the three can cover the space behind each of the other players on a through pass. Furthermore, four forwards attacking in a straight line across the field limit the passing possibilities.

As in any team game, the more than the players practice together, the better the system works. Each player must completely understand his role in the formation. Also, he must have a knowledge of the duties of the players around him. Only then can he be expected to function effectively as a member of the team.

WM Formation

One of the most basic offensive and defensive patterns for beginners is the WM formation. The three fullbacks and the wing halfbacks form the M; the W is formed by the insides, wingers, and center forward. This formation covers the field well and gives depth to the offense and defense.

In this formation the defensive coverage is comprised of fullbacks on the wingers, wing halfbacks covering the opposing inside man, and the center half or center fullback covering the center forward.

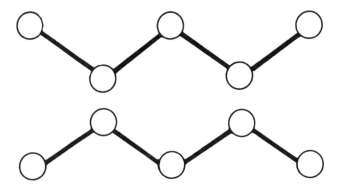

WM Formation

Inverted W Formation

Variations of this offensive pattern constitute the Invested W formation which retains the three-back defense. In this formation, the center forward assumes a position in line with the wingers. If the defense challenges with fullbacks on the wingers, halfbacks on the inside men, and the center half covering the center forward, the opposition is then in a defense which it is not accustomed to playing. It means the center half moves farther into the midfield and cannot play his "stopper " position. The fullbacks are pulled out of their normal positions and moved farther upfield to challenge the wingers. The halfbacks are now playing a "stopper role" because

Inverted W Formation

the opposing inside men are playing a double center forward position. All of this creates problems for the opposing defense. Intelligent forwards sometimes can capitalize on this situation before the other team can adjust.

4-2-4 Formation

The 4-2-4 formation became quite popular during the 1950s. For this formation use two midfield players who are quite gifted and who have a great deal of stamina, because they must attempt to control the entire middle of the field. The wing forwards should come deep into their defense to help when their team is defending, and the wing backs should move forward in support of the attack.

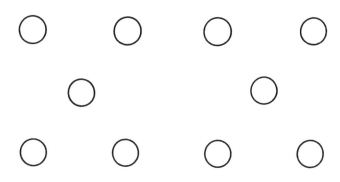

4-2-4 Formation

4-2-4 Formation
Using a Sweeper Back

A variation of a normal 4-2-4 formation is to use a sweeper back and only three men in the defensive back line. This provides the defense with additional support and cover and would also permit the use of a man-for-man defense.

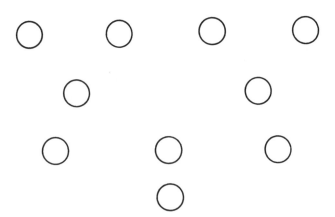

4-2-4 Formation Using a Sweeper Back

4-3-3 and 3-3-4
Formation

These two variations of the 4-2-4 are formed from that formation by moving one man to midfield from the four backs or the four forwards, depending on whether the team needs defensive or offensive strength.

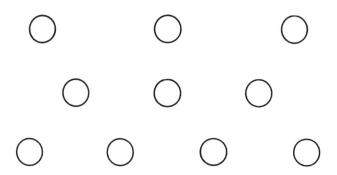

4-3-3 Formation

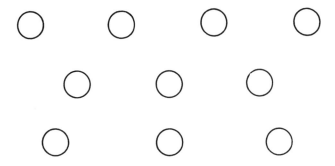

3-3-4 Formation

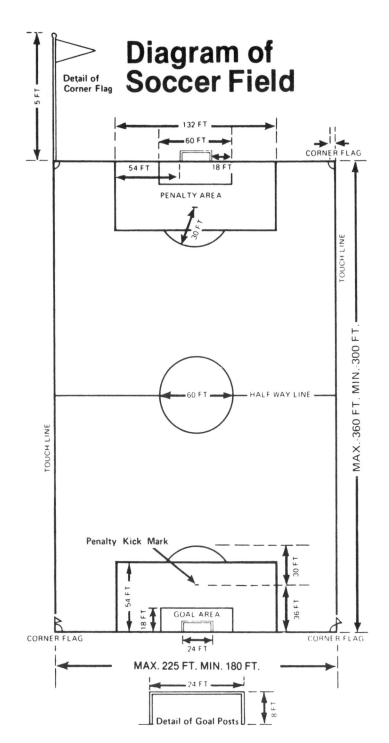

Diagram of Soccer Field

Detail of Corner Flag

5 FT

132 FT

60 FT

54 FT

18 FT

CORNER FLAG

PENALTY AREA

30 FT

TOUCH LINE

60 FT

HALF WAY LINE

MAX. 360 FT. MIN. 300 FT.

TOUCH LINE

Penalty Kick Mark

30 FT

54 FT

36 FT

18 FT

GOAL AREA

CORNER FLAG

24 FT

CORNER FLAG

MAX. 225 FT. MIN. 180 FT.

24 FT

8 FT

Detail of Goal Posts

Diagram of soccer field

Rules

Playing Rules

Laws of the Game

The definitive laws of the game of soccer are those of F.I.F.A., the "Federation International de Football Association," or, in English: the International Federation of Association Football. These laws apply all over the world and provide a standard which governs international competition.

The American Soccer League, Soccer Association for Youth, the United States Soccer Federation, the National Collegiate Athletic Association, and the Federation of State High School Associations all have their own set of laws, or rules, which basically conform to the F.I.F.A. laws, but which also have variations peculiar to each particular organization.

Various youth soccer programs also have made further changes to allow for problems specific to young players.

The F.I.F.A. laws of the game shall apply to play, except as may be amended in this book and which appear in bold type. The laws, as listed herein, are intended to change the nature of the game as little as possible, and are primarily directed toward creating a safer game for the participants, and providing means for all players to participate.

LAW ONE — THE FIELD OF PLAY

The field of play and appurtenances shall be as shown on the diagram.

1. Dimensions
Recommended field sizes are as follows:

Under 8:	**60 x 80 yards**
Under 10:	**60 x 90 yards**
Under 12:	**60 x 100 yards**
Under 14:	**65 x 110 yards**
Under 16 and Under 19:	**70 x 110 yards**

Wherever possible, the size of the field should be related to the age division using it.

2. Marking
    The field shall be marked with distinctive lines, not more than 5 inches in width. The longer lines shall be called the touch-lines, and the shorter lines the goal lines. (Marking must be with marble dust or latex paint, or some material which is not injurious to eyes or skin.)
        A halfway line shall be marked across the field of play. From the midpoint of this line, a 10-yard radius circle shall be marked.
        A flag on a post at least 5 feet high will be placed at each corner of the field. Similar flags may be used to mark mid-field, but must be at least 1 yard outside of the touchlines.

3. The Goal Area
    The goal area is marked by lines perpendicular to the goal line 6 yards into the field, and joined by a line parallel to the goal line.

4. The Penalty Area
    The penalty area is marked by lines perpendicular to the goal line 18 yards from each goalpost, extending 18 yards into the field, and joined by a line parallel to the goal line. A penalty-kick mark shall be made 12 yards from the goal line, opposite the center of the goal. From the penalty-kick mark, an arc of radius 10 yards shall be drawn outside the penalty area.

5. The Corner Area
    A quarter circle, or radius 1 yard, shall be drawn inside the four corners of the field.

6. The Goals
    The goals are placed at the midpoint of each goal line, with each upright the same distance from the corner flag, and 24 feet apart (inside measurement), joined by a crossbar 8 feet from the ground (lower edge). Uprights and crossbar should have the same width. Goal nets shall be attached to the posts and crossbar and fastened to the ground in such a manner as to not interfere with the goalie.

NOTES:

1. All markings are part of the areas they enclose.
2. Goals should be painted white.
3. Penalty areas, goal areas, and 10-yard circles are not to be reduced in size on smaller fields, nor is the goal size to be reduced from 8-foot by 24-foot inside measurements.

4. If a crossbar becomes damaged and falls, or is in danger of falling, it must be removed. League games man continue, with the approval of both coaches, with the referee's judgment determining whether any particular shot would have been under the crossbar, had one been there. However, tournament games will require that a solid crossbar be in place. Damage to the crossbar must be repaired, or the game moved to another field.

5. If the field is not adequately lined, the game will proceed, according to the best of the referees's ability to determine the position of the lines. If there are no nets on the goals, the game will proceed to the best of the referee's judgment.

6. A referee may refuse to start a game, or may stop it once play has started, if in the referee's judgment, the condition of the ground is such as to endanger the players. In the event of an electrical storm, play must be stopped until the danger has passed. If a game has been stopped after at least one-half has been played, and it cannot be re-started, it shall be considered an official game. If less than one-half has been played, it must be re-scheduled in its entirety.

LAW TWO — THE BALL

The ball shall be spherical; the outer casing shall be of leather or other approved material. No material shall be used which might be dangerous to the players.

Ages 6, 7 will use a No. 3 Ball, ages 7–11 will use a No. 4 Ball, ages 12–18 will use a No. 5 Ball.

The game ball will not be changed during the course of the game without the approval of the referees.

NOTES:

1. If the ball becomes deflated during play the game shall be stopped and re-started by dropping a new ball where the deflated ball was last played, but never inside the penalty area. (See "drop ball," Law Eight). If it is found to be deflated during a stoppage of the game it will be replaced and the game re-started normally

LAW THREE — PLAYERS AND SUBSTITUTIONS

A game will be played by two teams, each consisting of not more than eleven nor less than seven players, one of whom shall be the Goalkeeper. Each team shall designate one player as a Captain. If he or she leaves the game, another Captain must be designated. The active Captain is the only player permitted to discuss a rule interpretation with the referees.

Before all players on a team have completed playing their team required quarters (U–8 = 2, Others = 1), a team may substitute only for an injured or cautioned member of that team, and between quarters. Partial quarters played do not count toward fulfillment of personal required playing time, but do count toward the team's required playing time as it pertains to free substitutions. An ejected player may not be replaced; the team will play short for the remainder of the game. A player who was present at the start of the game and enters the game for the first time as a substitute for an injured or cautioned player must play another entire quarter (U–8 = 2 quarters) before the team achieves free substitution status.

During the progress of the game, the referees must be notified specifically before the Goalkeeper is changed, whether the change is made by means of another player on the field or by means of another player on the field or by means of a substitute from the sideline. When the Goalkeeper is changed between quarters, the referees need not be notified.

When all players of a team have completed their required playing time, the team has achieved "free substitution" status. For the remainder of the game, that team may substitute any number of players: On a goal kick, after a goal, during any extended time out (as for an injury), between quarters, and, by the team in possession, on a throw-in.

A player arriving late before or after the team has achieved "free substitution," must play the required personal time, or the remainder of the game. The "free substitution" status continues for the other players.

PENALTY: For illegal substitution, an indirect kick shall be awarded to the opposing team if the infraction is noted while the ball is in play, from the sport of the ball at that time. Whether or not the ball is in play, the entering player shall be cautioned.

LAW FOUR — PLAYERS' EQUIPMENT

A player shall not wear anything which is dangerous to himself or herself, or to another player. Players in all divisions shall wear gym, tennis, molded soccer shoes, or shoes with screw-in cleats. Metal or metal-tipped cleats are not allowed. The maximum length of a cleat is 3/4", the minimum width is 1/2" if individually mounted. If molded, and there are 10 or more cleats, the maximum length is 3/4" and the minimum width is 3/8".

The following shall be considered as illegal equipment, and as such shall not be worn by any player:

A. **Shinguards with exposed sharp edges.**
B. **Face or spectacle guards, helmets of any kind. Soft headwear, such as knit caps, is permitted. The Goalkeeper is permitted to wear a soft-billed cap.**
C. **Knee, head, thigh, or hip pads containing sole leather, fiber metal or any dangerous material, even though covered with soft padding.**
D. **Any cast of any type, even though covered with soft padding.**
E. **A knee brace may be worn, but shall be wrapped, and shall be approved by the referees.**
F. **Cleats with sharp edges.**
G. **Players shall not have any foreign objects in their mouths, such as gum or ice. Teeth guards are permitted.**

These rules shall not be waived even by agreement between both coaches and the referees.

All players on a team must wear shirts of the same identifying color. The Goalkeeper must wear a color different from that of either team.

It is the responsibility of the home team to change to a different color, if the two teams normally wear the same color.

Numbers of shirts are required, and must be different (...for each player), however, for non-tournament games when a team, because of a color conflict, must wear alternate shirts, such shirts need not be numbered.

PENALTY: If a player is wearing dangerous or illegal equipment, participation is forbidden until this is corrected to the satisfaction of the referee.

                     For an unresolved color conflict, the referees may permit the game to proceed, but the incident must be reported to the District Representative.

LAW FIVE—THE REFEREE

There shall be two referees, with equal jurisdiction. A single referee may be used in an emergency situation, with linesmen to assist only by indicating "out-of-bounds." Both referees shall have equal authority and responsibility in the calling of fouls and violations on any part of the field at any time.

The authority and the exercise of powers granted to referees by the Laws of the Game commence as soon as they enter the field of play. The power of penalizing shall extend to offenses committed when play has been temporarily suspended, or the ball is out of play. (A free kick may not be awarded if the ball is out of play when a foul is committed, but players may be cautioned or ejected).

A referee's decision on points of fact connected with the play shall be final.

The referee shall:

a. Enforce the laws.

b. Refrain from penalizing in cases where doing so would give an advantage to the offending team.

c. Act as game timekeeper, unless provision has been made by League or Tournament officials for sideline timekeeping. Time lost through accident or unusual delay is to be added.

d. Have the authority to stop the game for an infringement of the Laws, and to suspend or terminate the game if weather conditions or actions of spectators or players indicate that the stoppage is necessary. Such stoppage and the reasons therefore should be reported to the League administrator.

e. Caution any player guilty of misconduct, and eject the player if this is repeated. Ejections should be reported to the League administrator.

f. Allow no one other than the active players and linesmen to enter the field without permission.

g. Stop the game if a player is injured, but not during a drive on goal unless the injury appears to be serious. (The nearest referee is obliged to quickly check the condition of the injured play.) The referee only need have reason to believe that a player is seriously injured to stop the game, even if there is a drive on goal.

h. Eject any player who is guilty of violent conduct, serious foul play, or the use of abusive language.

i. Signal for the re-starting of the game after any stoppage. For the taking of kicks, the signal in U–8 and U–10 divisions must be with the whistle. For other divisions, the common practice throughout the world of allowing the kick to be taken as soon as the ball is properly placed, without a whistle, is to be followed. The referee may delay such a "quick" kick at his or her discretion. A second whistle may be given after a substitution, an extended time out, or for the taking of a penalty kick.

j. Use a drop ball to re-start game, after unresolved referee decisions, such as a whistle blown by mistake, or unknown team last touches out-of-bounds ball.

NOTES:

1. A referee may reverse a decision as long as play has not been re-started.
2. If the "advantage" clause has been applied, this decision cannot be revoked if the advantage is not realized.
3. Games may not be forfeited by referees. Conditions indicating a possible forfeit must be reported to the District Representative for a decision.
4. If a player or two players on the same team simultaneously commit two infringements, one of which calls for an indirect kick, and the other of which calls for a direct kick, a direct kick shall be awarded.
5. Coaching from the touchline during the course of the game shall be limited to verbal communication with the players of the coach's team. Megaphones, bullhorns, etc., may not be used. No coaching or comments shall be directed to the players or coaches of the opposing team.
6. During the course of the game, all coaches must remain on the side of the field, between the center line and the top of the penalty area (18-yard line) where the team's substitutes are situated.

> **PENALTY:** For violation of Law Five notes 5 or 6 — After receiving one caution, the offending coach shall be ejected form the playing field.

LAW SIX — LINESMEN

The duties of linesmen shall be limited to indicating to the referee when a ball goes out-of-bounds.

LAW SEVEN — DURATION OF THE GAME

All games will be played in quarters with a kick-off to begin each quarter. The team that kicks off in the 1st quarter will kick off in the 3rd quarter. The team that kicks off in the 2nd quarter will kick off in the 4th quarter. Teams will change ends at the end of each quarter. Times of quarters will be:

Ages 6, 7   10 minutes

Ages 8–11   15 minutes

Ages 12–18   20 minutes

Intervals between quarters will be one minute; half time interval will be 10 minutes.

Allowances shall be made within each period for time lost through accident or other cause, the amount of which shall be at the discretion of the referee. This time may not be added to a different period.

Time shall be extended only to permit the taking of a penalty kick which was awarded before time ran out. Time may not be extended for the taking of other free kicks.

Play ends exactly at the instant that time runs out, regardless of the position or motion of the ball at that time.

LAW EIGHT — THE START OF PLAY

At the beginning of the game, choice of ends and the kick-off shall be decided by the toss of a coin. The team winning the toss shall choose an end or the kick-off; the team losing the toss will receive the remaining choice.

Upon the referee's signal, the game is started by a player taking a placekick (i.e., a kick at the ball while it is stationary on the ground at mid-field) into the opponent's half of the field. The players of each team must be in their team's half of the field until the ball is kicked. Opposing players must remain 10 yards from the ball until it is kicked.

As in all free kicks, the ball is not in play until it has travelled the distance of its own circumference, and the kicker may not play the ball a second time until it has been touched by another play, or either team.

For violation of the above provisions, the kick must be re-taken, except for the case where the kicker plays the ball a second time, the kick-off otherwise having been legal. In that case, an indirect kick is awarded to the opposing team.

A goal may not be scored direct from a kick-off.

After a goal has been scored, the game is re-started in a like manner, by the team scored against.

After a game has been stopped while the ball was in play, as for an injury, it is re-started with a drop ball. The referee shall drop the ball where it was when play was stopped, and it shall be in play when it touches the ground. If the ball was in play within a penalty area and not in possession of the Goalkeeper when the stoppage occurred, it shall be dropped at the nearest point outside the penalty area. If the ball was in clear possession of the Goalkeeper when the stoppage occurred, play will be re-started with an indirect free kick taken by the Goalkeeper's team at the place where it was when the stoppage occurred, and in accordance with Law Thirteen. **In the U–8 division, a kick taken under these circumstances will be taken from a point 12 yards from the goal line if the ball was not at least 12 yards from the goal line when the stoppage occurred.**

LAW NINE — BALL IN AND OUT OF PLAY

The ball is out of play when it has completely crossed the goal line or touchline, whether on the ground or in the air, and when the game has been stopped by the referee.

The ball is in play at all other times, including:

1. If it rebounds onto the field from a goalpost, crossbar, or corner flag.
2. If it strikes the referee or linesman on the field of play.
3. If there is an apparent infringement, but no signal has been given by the referee.

LAW TEN — METHOD OF SCORING

Except as otherwise provided by these Laws, a goal is scored when the whole of the ball has passed over the goal line, between the goalposts, and under the crossbar.

A goal is not allowed if the ball has been thrown, carried, or intentionally propelled by hand or arm by a player of the attacking team, other than the attacking team's goalie throwing from his own penalty area.

The team scoring more goals shall be the winner; if there are no goals, or an equal number of goals are scored by each team, the game shall be a draw.

NOTES:

1. A goal may not be allowed if the ball has not crossed the goal line. If the ball is stopped by an outside agency (e.g., a dog, or spectator), it must be dropped, at the nearest point outside the penalty area.
2. The referee must not award a goal unless in a position to observe and be certain that the ball has completely crossed the goal line.
3. A goal may not be allowed if the ball touches a foreign agency before entering the goal (dog, spectator, etc.) The referee is not a foreign agency.

LAW ELEVEN — OFF-SIDE

A player is off-side if nearer the opponent's goal line than the ball at the moment the ball is played toward the player by a teammate, unless:
1. The player is in his or her own half of the field of play.
2. There are at least two opponents nearer to their goal line.
3. The ball is received directly from a goal kick, corner kick, throw-in, or drop ball.

> PENALTY: An indirect free kick by the opposing team, from the place where the infringement occurred, unless the offense is committed by a player in the opponents' goal area, in which case the free kick shall be taken from a point anywhere within that half of the goal area in which the offense occurred (or 12-yard line for U–8).

> NOTE: It is stressed that off-side is determined at the instant the ball is passed by a teammate to the player in an off-side position. The position of the player when the ball is received has no bearing on off-side.

A player in an off-side position shall not be penalized unless interfering with the play or with an opponent, or able to gain an advantage by being in an off-side position.

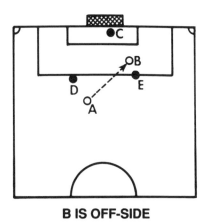

B IS OFF-SIDE

1. CLEAR PASS TO ONE ON SAME SIDE

(A) has run the ball up, and having (D) in front, passes to (B). (B) is off-side because he is in front of (A) and there are not two opponents between him and the goal line when the ball is passed by (A).

If (B) waits for (E) to fall back before he shoots, this will not put him on-side, because it does not alter his position with relation to (A) at the moment the ball was passed by (A).

2. CLEAR PASS TO ONE OF SAME SIDE

(Continued)

(A) has run the ball up, and having (D) in front, passes across the field. (B) runs from position 1 to position 2. (B) is not off-side because at the moment the ball was passed by (A) he was not in front of the ball, and had two opponents between him and the goal line.

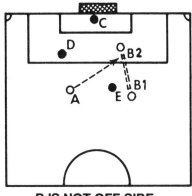

B IS NOT OFF-SIDE

3. CLEAR PASS TO ONE OF SAME SIDE

(Continued)

(A) and (B) make a passing run up the wing. (A) passes the ball to (B), who can not shoot because he has (D) in front. (A) then runs from position 1 to position 2 at which time (B) passes the ball to him. (A) is off-side because he is in front of the ball and he had not two opponents between him and the goal line when the ball was played by (B).

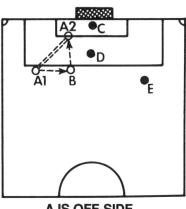

A IS OFF-SIDE

4. RUNNING BACK FOR BALL

(A) centers the ball. (B) runs back from position 1 to position 2, and then dribbles between (D) and (E) and scores. (B) is off-side because he is in front of the ball and he had not two opponents between him and the goal line at the moment the ball was played by (A).

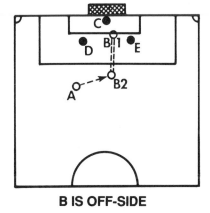

B IS OFF-SIDE

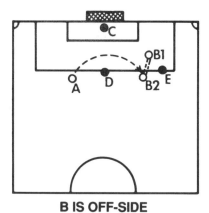

B IS OFF-SIDE

5. RUNNING BACK FOR BALL
(Continued)
(A) Makes a high shot at goal, and the wind and screw carry the ball back. (B) runs from position 1 to position 2 and scores. (B) is off-side because he is in front of the ball and he had not two opponents between him and the goal line at the moment the ball was last played by (A).

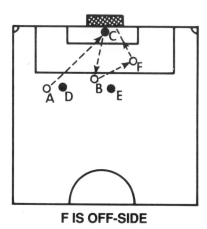

F IS OFF-SIDE

6. SHOT AT GOAL RETURNED BY GOALKEEPER
(A) shoots at goal. The ball is played by (C) and (B) obtains possession but slips and passes the ball to (F), who scores. (F) is off-side because he is in front of (B), and when the ball was passed by (B) he had not two opponents between him and the goal line.

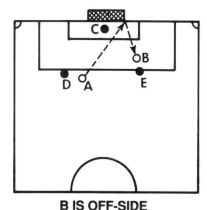

B IS OFF-SIDE

7. BALL REBOUNDING FROM GOALPOSTS OR CROSSBAR
(A) shoots for goal and the ball rebounds from the goalpost into play. (B) secures the ball and scores. (B) is off-side because the ball is last played by (A), a player of his own side, and when (A) played it (B) was in front of the ball and did not have two opponents between him and the goal line.

8. BALL REBOUNDING FROM GOALPOSTS OR CROSSBAR

(A) shoots for goal and the ball rebounds from the crossbar into play. (A) follows up from position 1 to position 2, and then passes (B) who has run up on the other side. (B) is off-side because the ball is last played by (A), a player of his own side, and when (A) played it (B) was in front of the ball and did not have two opponents between him and the goal line. If (A) had scored himself at the second attempt, instead of passing (B), it would have been a goal.

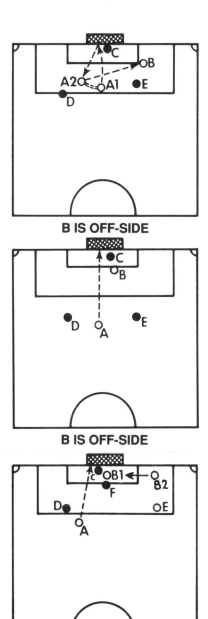

B IS OFF-SIDE

9. OBSTRUCTING THE GOAL-KEEPER

(A) shoots for goal and scores. (B) however, obstructs (C) so that he cannot get at the ball. The goal must be disallowed, because (B) is in an off-side position and may not touch the ball himself, nor in any way whatever interfere with an opponent.

B IS OFF-SIDE

10. OBSTRUCTING THE GOAL-KEEPER

(A) shoots for goal. (B) runs from position 2 to position 1 while the ball is in transit and prevents (C) from playing it properly. (B) is off-side because he is in front of (A) and has not two opponents between him and the goal line when (A) plays the ball. When in this position (B) may not touch the ball himself, nor in any way whatever interfere with an opponent.

B IS OFF-SIDE

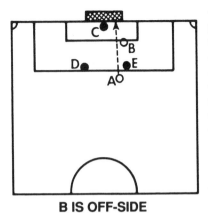

B IS OFF-SIDE

11. OBSTRUCTING AN OPPONENT OTHER THAN THE GOALKEEPER

(A) shoots for goal. (B) prevents (E) from running in to intercept the ball (B) is off-side because he is in front of (A) and has not two opponents between him and the goal line when (A) plays the ball. When in this position (B) may not touch the ball himself, nor in any way whatever interfere with an opponent.

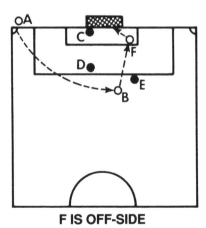

F IS OFF-SIDE

12. AFTER A CORNER KICK

(A) takes a corner kick and the ball goes to (B). (B) shoots for goal and as the ball is passing through, (F) deflects it into the goal. (F) is off-side because after the corner kick has been taken, the ball is last played by (B), a player of his own side, and when (B) played it (F) was in front of the ball and has not two opponents between him and the goal line.

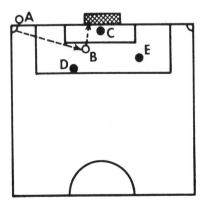

B IS NOT OFF-SIDE

13. AFTER A CORNER KICK

(Continued)
(A) takes a corner kick and the ball goes to (B), who puts it through goal. (B) has only one opponent between him and the goal line, but he is not off-side because a player cannot be off-side directly from a corner kick.

14. AFTER A CORNER KICK
(Continued)
(A) takes a corner kick and (D) attempts to kick it upfield, but miskicks and the ball goes to (B), who puts it through goal. (B) is not off-side because the ball was last played by an opponent, (D).

B IS NOT OFF-SIDE

15. AFTER A THROW-IN FROM THE TOUCHLINE
(A) throws to (B) and then runs from touchline to position 2. (B) passes the ball to (A) in position 2. (A) is off-side because he is in front of the ball and has not two opponents between him and the goal line when the ball is passed forward to him by (B).

A IS OFF-SIDE

16. AFTER A THROW-IN FROM THE TOUCHLINE (Continued)
(A) throws the ball to (B). Although (B) is in front of the ball and has not two opponents between him and the goal line, he is not off-side because a player cannot be off-side from a throw-in.

B IS NOT OFF-SIDE

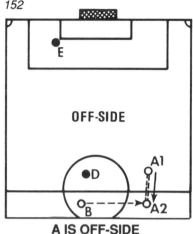

A IS OFF-SIDE

17. A PLAYER CANNOT PUT HIMSELF ON-SIDE BY RUNNING BACK INTO HIS OWN HALF OF THE FIELD OF PLAY.

If (A) is in his opponents' half of the field of play, and is off-side in position when (B) last played the ball, he cannot put himself on-side by moving back into his own half of the field of play.

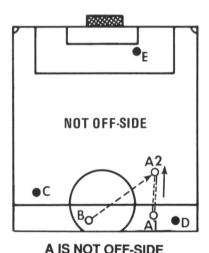

A IS NOT OFF-SIDE

18. A PLAYER WITHIN HIS OWN HALF OF THE FIELD OF PLAY IS NOT OFF-SIDE WHEN HE ENTERS HIS OPPONENTS' HALF OF THE FIELD OF PLAY.

LAW TWELVE — FOULS AND MISCONDUCT

The intentional commission of any of the following offenses will result in the award of a direct free kick to the opposing team, at the point of the offense, **unless the offense is committed by a player in the opponents's goal area, in which case the free kick shall be taken from a point anywhere within that half of the goal area in which the offense occurred (or 12-yard line for U–8).** If the offense be by a member of the defending team within its own penalty area, a penalty kick will be awarded.

For the following offenses, penalties may be awarded only if the ball was in play at the time of the offense, but the position of the ball is irrelevant, except, of course, in the case of a hand ball.

1. Kicking or attempting to kick an opponent.
2. Tripping or attempted tripping, with leg or body.
3. Jumping at an opponent.
4. Charging an opponent from behind.
5. Striking or attempting to strike an opponent.
6. Holding an opponent.
7. Pushing an opponent, with hand or arm.
8. Charging an opponent in a violent or dangerous manner. (A fair charge requires that both players have at least one foot on the ground, and that contact be shoulder-to-shoulder).
9. **Carrying, striking, or propelling the ball with hand or arm (except for a goalkeeper within his or her own penalty area). Girls may protect their chests from the impact of the ball by holding their arms against their chests, but any movement of the arm toward the ball will be called a "hand ball."**
10. Charging a goalkeeper in the goal area or where goalkeeper is in possession of the ball in penalty area.
11. **A sliding tackle made from outside the peripheral vision of the opponent in possession of the ball (the rear 180 degrees) will be considered tripping, even if first contact is with the ball. If no contact is made with either player or ball. It will be called "dangerous play," with an indirect kick awarded.**
12. Attempting to kick a ball while in possession of the goalkeeper. Possession is having control, even if only with one hand.

> **NOTE:** **Charging of the goalkeeper in the goal area or in possession of the ball, or attempting to kick a ball in the goalkeeper's possession must be punished by a caution or ejection, the choice to be subject to the referee's judgment.**

The commission of any of the following offenses will result in the award of an indirect free kick, taken by the opposing team at the point of infringement:

1. Playing in a manner which could result in injury to the player or to any other player. Examples of dangerous play are: (a) raising the foot, in an attempt to play the ball, to the

level of an opponent's chest or higher when the opponent is in a normal position, or (b) using a double kick (scissors, bicycle, or hitch kick) within six feet of an opponent, or (c) lowering the head to the level of the waist or lower in an attempt to head the ball in the presence of an oncoming player, or (d) playing or attempting to play the ball while lying on the ground within six feet of an opponent. "Dangerous Play" is always a judgment call, which is made at the discretion of the referee. These examples are not exclusive. They are for illustration only and are not meant to limit the use of discretion by the referee.

2. Charging fairly when the ball is not within playing distance of the players concerned.

3. When not playing the ball, interposing the body so as to obstruct an opponent's movement.

4. Improper clearing of the ball by the Goalkeeper. The following rules shall apply:

> **U–8 and U–10 Goalkeepers may run with the ball and take any number of steps while inside the penalty area, as long as there is no excessive delay in clearing the ball.**
>
> **All U–12 and older division Goalkeepers may not take more than four steps while in clear possession before releasing the ball so that it is played by another player. "Clear Possession" shall include holding, bouncing, or throwing the ball in the air and catching it.**

5. Excessive delay in clearing the ball by the Goalkeeper.

A player who enters or leaves the field without the referee's permission shall be cautioned. If the game is stopped to administer this caution, the game will be re-started by an indirect kick taken by the opposing team at the point where this player was when the game was stopped, or where the offense was committed. That also applies to too many players on the field.

A caution shall be administered also:

1. If a player persistently infringes the Laws of the Game.

2. If dissent is shown by word or action with any decision of the referee.

A caution may be administered for:

1. Unsportsmanlike conduct.

2. Foul language.

These also require that an indirect kick be awarded to the opposing team from the point of the offense.

A player will be ejected from the game for:
1. Violent conduct or serious foul play.
2. The use of abusive language.
3. A second offense requiring a caution.

If the game is stopped to eject the player, no other Law having been infringed, an indirect kick shall be awarded to the opposing team from the point of the offense.

NOTE:

1. If a goalkeeper throws the ball vigorously at an opponent, or pushes with the ball while holding it, the referee shall award a penalty kick, provided that the offense took place in the penalty area.
2. The referee need not stop the game to administer a caution: the advantage clause may be invoked. The caution will be administered as soon as play stops.
3. As attempt to prevent a throw-in being taken or to prevent the Goalkeeper from clearing the ball is unsportsmanlike conduct.

LAW THIRTEEN — FREE KICK

There are two types of free kicks: Direct, from which a goal can be scored direct against the offending team, and indirect, from which a goal cannot be scored unless the ball has been touched after the kick by any other player, of either team, before it enters the goal.

When a free kick is being taken by a defending team from inside its own penalty area, all opposing players must be outside the penalty area and at least 10 yards from the ball. To be in play, the ball must travel the distance of its own circumference and beyond the penalty area. It may not be kicked back to the goalkeeper to be cleared. A free kick which does not pass beyond the penalty area must be re-taken.

Any free kick awarded to a defending team inside its own goal area may be taken from any point within that half of the goal area in which the free kick has been awarded **(or 12-yard line for U–8).**

When a free kick is being taken outside the kicker's own penalty area, it may be kicked in any direction. Players of the opposing team should be 10 yards from the ball and must be at least 10 yards from the ball if requested by the kicker or referee, except in the case of an indirect kick being taken within less than 10 yards of the opponent's goal. In this case, defending players may stand on the goalline, between the goalposts. On all free kicks, the ball is not in play until it has travelled the distance of its own circumference. If players of the opposing side encroach into the penalty area, or within 10 yards of the ball, the referee may delay the taking of the kick until the Law is complied with. Encroachment is to be treated as unsportsmanlike conduct. The ball must be stationary when the kick is taken, and the kicker may not play the ball again until it has been touched by another player.

PENALTY: For playing the ball twice, an indirect kick is awarded to the opposing team at the point where it was played the second time.

For delaying the taking of a kick by encroachment or attempts at distracting the kicker, a caution shall be given.

LAW FOURTEEN — PENALTY KICK

A penalty kick is taken from the penalty mark, which is opposite the center of the goal and 12 yards from the goal line.

When the kick is taken, all players other than the player taking the kick and the opposing Goalkeeper shall be within the field of play but outside the penalty area, and at least 10 yards from the ball.

The Goalkeeper must stand on the goal line, between the goalposts, and may not lift or slide either foot until the ball is kicked. Movement of the body or arms is permitted.

The kick must be forward, and may not be played a second time by the kicker until touched by another player. The ball must travel the distance of its circumference before it is in play. A goal may be scored direct from a penalty kick.

When a penalty kick is being taken during the normal course of play, or when time has been extended at the end of a period to allow a penalty kick to be taken or re-taken, a goal shall not be nullified if, before passing between the posts and under crossbar, the ball touches either or both of the goalposts, or the crossbar, or the Goalkeeper, or any combination of these agencies, providing that no other infringement has occurred. On a kick taken after time has expired, the kicker may not play the ball a second time.

PENALTY: 1. For any infringement of this Law by the defending team, the kick is re-taken if a goal is not scored. Goal is allowed if scored.
2. For any infringement of the Law by the attacking team, the kick is re-taken if a goal is scored.

If a goal is not scored and the ball out of play, continue the game as is normal. However, if the Goalkeeper deflects the ball out-of-bounds, or it is rebounds into play, play is stopped and an indirect kick is awarded to the defending team.

3. If the kicker is guilty of an infringement after the ball is in play, play is stopped and an indirect kick is awarded to the defending team.

4. If both teams infringe, the kick is re-taken whether or not it scored.

NOTES:

1. The penalty kick may not be taken until the signal to do so is given by the referee. This signal will not be given until all players are in position in accordance with the Law.

2. The kick shall be taken even if an infringement is noted by the referee after giving the signal for the kick. A decision will then be made in accordance with the Law, depending on the outcome of the kick.

LAW FIFTEEN — THROW-IN

When the whole of the ball has passed over the touchline, either on the ground or in the air, it shall be put into play by a throw-in in any direction at the point where it crossed the line, by a player of the team opposite to that of the player who last touched it.

The thrower at the moment of delivering the ball must face the field of play with both feet on or outside the touchline and part of each foot in contact with the ground. The thrower shall use both hands equally and shall deliver the ball from behind and over his head. The ball shall be in play immediately as it enters the field of play, but the thrower shall not again play the ball until it has been touched by another player.

A goal may not be scored direct from a throw-in.

The off-side law does not apply at the taking of a throw-in.

PENALTY: 1. For an improper throw-in, it shall be taken by the other team.

2. For playing the ball a second time, an indirect kick by the opposing team at the point of the offense.

LAW SIXTEEN — GOAL KICK

When the ball passes completely over the defending team's goal line, and was last touched by an attacking player, and a goal was not scored, it is put into play by an indirect kick by the defending team, taken from a point within that half of the goal area nearest to where it crossed the line. **In the U–8 the kick may be taken from in front of the goal area, up to 12 yards from the goal line.**

All provisions of the Laws regarding free kicks from a defending team's penalty area apply, except that the off-side Law does not apply at the taking of the kick.

LAW SEVENTEEN — CORNER KICK

When the ball passes completely over the defending team's goal line, and was last touched by a defending player, and a goal has not been scored, it is put into play by a direct kick, taken by a player of the attacking team from the corner of the field nearest to where the ball crossed the line. The ball must be placed within the quarter circle, or no more than 2 yards from both the touchline and goal line.

The corner flag may not be moved for the taking of the corner kick. A goal may be scored direct from a corner kick.

Defending players must remain 10 yards from the ball until it is in play, that is, has travelled the distance of its own circumference. The kicker may not play the ball a second time until it has been touched by another player.

The off-side Law does not apply at the taking of the kick.

> PENALTY: For playing the ball a second time, an indirect kick will be awarded the defending team at the point of the offense.

DANGEROUS PLAY

**GOALKEEPER
CARRYING BALL**

Playing Signals

GOAL

INDIRECT KICK

TIME OUT

CORNER KICK

PLAY ON

GOAL KICK

RED CARD—EJECTION

YELLOW CARD—CAUTION

SAVE: The deflection or catching of a ball by the goalkeeper to prevent a goal.

STRIKER: A central attacking forward.

SWEEPER: A free back behind the last line of defenders.

TACKLING: Technique used to dispossess an opponent of the ball.

THROW-IN: The means of putting the ball back into play after it goes out of bounds over the touchline.

TOUCHLINE: The side boundaries of the field.

TRAPPING: Bringing the ball under control and stopping it.

WING: A forward who generally positions himself and plays near the side boundaries of the field.

Index